Timberline Trees: McClure Meadows
1938. Carbon pencil

John W Winkley

Bay View 1913

I was born in Vienna in 1894; arrived in New York at the age of 16½, alone. It took me several years of insistence on my part to have my parents (one of them) to give in and let me realize my dream to visit America for one year and see the Indians, and see the Wild West, then return and finish my schooling on the hard benches of the Schotten Gymnasium.

It was a different America that received me and when the year was gone, the finest team of Percherons could not have dragged me back to that restricted circle in Vienna. Fortunately I was well supplied with plenty of money and could indulge in any whim that captured my fancy of the moment.

By a freak of chance I came to San Francisco and it was a sheer accident that I enrolled in the San Francisco Institute of Art where I studied drawing and painting under Professor [Frank] van Sloun for a number of years. I shall always remember him with the greatest affection and gratitude.

The early prints of San Francisco were all made, beginning in the second year at school, after school hours on the crowded streets of San Francisco. . . .

Holographic fragment, written
for the May, 1955 exhibit at
Kunstzaal Binsbergen,
Arnhem, Holland

To J W Winkler from E.R. Humphry
May 1918
1918

MASTER OF LINE
John W. Winkler—American Etcher

by Mary Millman and Dave Bohn

CAPRA PRESS
SANTA BARBARA

Library of Congress Cataloging-in-Publication Data
Millman, Mary.
    Master of line : John Winkler, American etcher / by Mary Millman and Dave Bohn.
        p.   cm.
    Includes bibliographical references and index.
    ISBN 0-88496-358-6 :
    1. Winkler, John William, 1894-1979—Biography.   2. Etchers—United States—Biography.
    3. Winkler, John William, 1894-1979—Catalogs.   I. Winkler, John William, 1894-1979.
    II. Bohn, Dave.   III. Title.
    NE2012.W55M55   1994
    769.92—dc20
[B]   94-5208
                                                                       CIP

Published by Capra Press
P.O. Box 2068   Printed in Japan
Santa Barbara CA 93120   First Edition

Irmgard 1917

This book is for John W. Winkler, master of line
and carver-in-wood extraordinary
— and to Elizabeth Ginno Winkler (1907–1991)
and John Aronovici.

*T*ABLE OF CONTENTS

Hang Far Lo c.1913

Busy Street in Chinatown c.1915

Stockton Street Tunnel 1915

INTRODUCTION. . . . that is, being drawn by the particular image into a contemplation of the grandeur of the art of etching itself. Like others before me, I came to see that Winkler's etched images are distinguished by this remarkable power.

The scope of this volume necessarily exceeds the realm of John William Winkler's etched works in order to follow the remarkable evolution of his intense, albeit often private, artistic life. But for a very significant portion of Winkler's career, in the public eye he embodied the American form of a European prototype known to scholarship as the "painter-etcher." In the vanguard of a graphic art movement sometimes called the "second revival" of American etching—roughly 1910–1929—a painter-etcher's work was admired to the degree that it suppressed all visual traces of those messy and laborious methods by which it was produced, and projected the impression that the artist, swept by the feeling of the moment, had spontaneously rendered the scene. Within the borders of an etching plate Winkler had no peer in the creation of this illusive quality.

To appreciate even the simplest etched work, a viewer needs to have firmly in mind the rudiments of the process by which the etcher translates a mental image into a picture in ink on paper. In general, printmaking media are complex and often technically difficult modes of visual expression compared to relatively direct media such as painting or drawing. The art of etching, however, carries the inherent complexity of printmaking to such a dimension that, in the hands of all but the most skilled craftspersons, it is more likely to defeat expression than to enable or enhance it.

———————————

When, now some years ago, I began to work with Winkler's etchings, I responded to the energy and apparent spontaneity of the images which, in my eyes, were always gently tinted by his pervasive humor. But it took me quite a while to experience first-hand the sensation reported by Winkler's etching revival colleagues—that is, being drawn by the particular image into a contemplation of the grandeur of the art of etching itself. Like others before me, I came to see that Winkler's etched images are distinguished by this remarkable power. If you take them at face value and pass some quiet time in their company they will, without intrusion, educate you and assume a cherished place in your life experience.

Across the more than eighty years of Winkler's life, many individuals recognized the quality of the man and the power of his work. One after another of these people took it upon themselves to assist him by forwarding his artistic cause according to their own means, and in some sense this volume might be understood as the most recent of such endeavors. Many of the above have been acknowledged in the text: Bertha Jaques, John Taylor Arms, Arthur Heintzelman, Louis Godefroy, Nora Crowe Winkler, Elizabeth Ginno Winkler, and Marci Thomas. But our story passes by several such persons because they encountered Winkler toward the end, when etching was culturally insignificant and Winkler himself was preoccupied with other projects.

William DuBois, together with his wife and partner, Ida Mae, served collectively as Winkler's first Boswell. They met him in the 1940s when he was thoroughly dug in at the decaying "Mediterranean" mansion known as the "plaster palace," and when the state of his enormous sun-flooded studio was several leagues beyond the normal frightful mess. Then in 1971, motivated by genuine friendship and an informed admiration for Winkler's etchings they plunged full-time into the chaos, determined to restore order. Undeterred by the curmudgeonly resistance behind which Winkler had lain low for decades, Bill and Ida Mae started by asking simple questions, such as "When did you etch this, how many states are there for this plate, was this needled on site, was this etched on zinc or copper?" More often than not they got answers, and so they persisted, hoping to uncover and document the inherent order of production. Nor does it detract from the success of their efforts to know that by this time Winkler himself had garbled or forgotten a great deal of his own history. Finally, in 1974, Bill and Ida Mae wrote and produced the catalogue for the Winkler retrospective at the California Palace of the Legion of Honor, curated by Fenton Kastner of the Achenbach Foundation for Graphic Arts. Bill DuBois passed away in 1984, but Ida Mae's unstinting generosity and enthusiasm were fundamental to the conception and research upon which this volume is based.

And then, Jack Ford. During much of the time Bill and Ida Mae were *upstairs* in the studio, Ford was in the *basement* printing Winkler's old copper plates. Beyond the contribution of his own printing expertise — some of it gained through Winkler's tutelage — Ford has said, "I was Wink's eyes." Which means that by the 1970s Winkler's vision could not sustain the required focus. So twice a week for about eight years Ford played apprentice to the master, producing a second run of prints, each of which had to satisfy tyrannical standards. Ford's devotion to the great etcher and the project at hand assured the survival of the integrity of Winkler's etched corpus.

———————————

To the numerous persons who contributed to the substantive research upon which this work stands, Dave Bohn and I express our warmest thanks: especially to Dr. Joseph Baird, Jr., Gary Breitweiser, Philip Choy, Douglas Grant, Deborah Lovely (Lovely Fine Arts, Oakbrook Terrace, Illinois), Dr. John Whitten of Vienna, Alain de Janvry, Annette Herskowitz, Dan Johnston at UC-Berkeley Library Photographic Service, Ann Gilbert — UC-Berkeley Art Librarian, and John Aronovici for the trust and cooperation as keeper of the Winkler Archives.

Readers of the manuscript stages included Peter Solomon, William Schwarz, Nancy Carleton, Judith Sanders, and Elizabeth Ginno Winkler. We thank them for their critical commentary. And we are grateful to George and Lynne Jensen of Gustavus, Alaska, and Hilary and Daniel Goldstine of Berkeley for providing layout workspace.

Special thanks to the libraries and archives that helped us unearth the numerous pieces of Winkler's public career: the Bancroft and Environmental Design libraries at UC-Berkeley; the California State Library, the Los Angeles County Museum of Art library, the Anne Bremmer Library at the San Francisco Art Institute, the Archives of American Art in San Francisco, the Boston Public Library (Microtext Department), the Brooklyn Museum library (Deborah Wythe, Archivist), and the College of Wooster Art Museum (Kitty McManus Zurko, Curator).

And finally, gratitude to my longtime bibliophiliac and literary doppelgänger, Dave Bohn, who came to love Winkler's work as much as he enjoyed his quixotic Austrian neighbor. *Mary Millman, Berkeley*

1. 'lo, folks !

The man known to the world of early twentieth century American graphic art as John William Winkler first appeared in the city of San Francisco in 1912. After a brief and (he always insisted) innocent stay at a waterfront bordello, he was ushered to the home of the Nelson family, at 1822 Bush Street, by a benevolent local attorney who came upon him furiously smoking cigars at a penny arcade near the Hall of Justice. No doubt intrigued by the contrast between Winkler's expensive, impeccable attire and the seedy surroundings, the attorney had apparently selected this particular idle youth for a dose of badly needed guidance.

Shortly after Winkler took up respectable lodgings on Bush Street, he chanced upon the entrance to the San Francisco Institute of Art, housed in a new structure replacing its original home in Mark Hopkins' hunting lodge which the 1906 earthquake had leveled. The sign beckoned him and on impulse, Winkler later said, he entered immediately— immediately after demanding assurance from the receptionist that it would take only three months to attain the cartooning skills that had enabled Charles Dana Gibson to make a million dollars.[1] (Winkler had always drawn pictures to amuse himself, so without hesitation he decided that day to become a cartoonist. If this has the ring of pure fiction, consider the *San Francisco City Directory* of 1912, which lists John Winkler at 1822 Bush Street as "Cartoonist." And consider further the very first drawing in his art school sketchbook—the self-portrait of a beaming young man, clutching his portfolio and leaning against a pencil that doubles for a lamppost, entitled *'lo, folks!*) Thus Winkler enrolled at the San Francisco Institute of Art on November 1, 1912,[2] hoping that he could make a name and a fortune for himself with his pencil.

Of Winkler's life prior to the Institute very little is known and almost nothing can be documented or verified. The responsibility for our ignorance rests squarely with the artist, for he refused to offer accurate information about his early years, and without any apparent compunction mystified his past with a seemingly inexhaustible supply of tales. He concealed his identity from family and friends alike, taking his birthname with him to the grave.[3] But he did all this with a characteristic brand of humor, distilling from private sources a collection of stories which, taken together over the years, comprised a self-legend worthy of an aristocratic European adventurer in the New World.

The story, as told by Winkler, begins in Vienna prior to the turn of the century, where he was born to a family of considerable status and ancient wealth. He said his father had been one of Franz Josef's "paper generals," but whether Winkler intended derision by this remark is impossible to tell. He was the younger of two brothers, failed to demonstrate an inclination for the illustrious military future that his parents desired for their sons, and was disfavored because he was physically a "runt." His most vivid childhood memories came from visits with his grandmother who managed the family estates in the north of Austria, close to the Czech border. There he was free from the social restraints of Vienna, and as lord of the manor could lead the village boys or taunt them. He rather regularly got into a great deal of mischief, but in retrospect he loved his own irreverence and smiled on his doting grandmother, who was always willing to pay off a peasantry irate over his vandalism.

Winkler's family required that he attend the *gymnasium*, to educate and prepare him for the government position they knew they could secure for him. They did not see, and most likely did not care, how deeply his heart recoiled at the bureaucratic future they insisted upon. By this time, certain that adventure awaited him, his imagination had been wholly captured by the vision of a wild and unfettered America—the America of cowboys and tramps that revealed itself on every page of his dime novels, volumes he was constrained to store with a friend because his father had banished them from the household.[4] At odds with his environment, Winkler cast about for a way out of the society that bound him. He attempted to enlist in the Austrian navy—it should have been easy since his uncle was an admiral—but was rejected because of poor eyesight, thus ending his fantasy of traveling to Sumatra, there to jump ship and confront destiny in the tropics. At one point, and without much fore-thought, he boarded a train bound for a western European port where he intended to book passage to America. His father caught wind of it and arranged for the German authorities to intercept and detain him, perhaps in Hamburg. Confined to a rail compartment, he was returned without ceremony to Vienna.

But the issue of escape did not end there. Instead, resolve solidified. His vision of America became an obsession and, by Winkler's account, he nagged and hounded his family for permission to go. His father never gave consent but his mother and grandmother relented, offering a conditional arrangement by which he would take a one-year leave of absence from the *gymnasium* to travel in America, and would then return to Vienna to finish his education. In furtherance of this venture they allowed him to be outfitted by the family tailor, who was persuaded to fashion the outrageous chrome yellow suit Winkler demanded—with wide lapels "like real Americans wore"—on the abject pretext that he needed it for *eine Maskerade*. He purchased flamboyant shoes at the Salamander shoe store, a venerable establishment which is still in business in Vienna. Thus equipped with the proper attire for wild America, having purchased a telescope for the ocean journey, and carrying his grandmother's gift of $5,000 in his pocket, Winkler embarked on the great adventure to meet hobos, Indians, and especially Buffalo Bill—all this at age sixteen. (Late in life, when Winkler ruminated on these events, he said they appeared to him as if in a dream. He audibly wondered at the pure romanticism of his own actions, but also expressed pride in his early courage.)

Whether from the beginning Winkler intended to disregard the one-year agreement with his mother, or whether having reached America he entered into its ethos so thoroughly that he could not bring himself to return to Vienna, it is certain that he never saw Austria again nor, according to his account, ever again communicated with his family. He did say that in the mid-1920s, when he and his wife were residing in Paris, he engaged a detective agency to locate his parents. Although he had not made a million dollars, he had by then achieved an international reputation as a fine artist and a master etcher, and perhaps felt he could face his family free from the gnawing differences which seem to have clouded his child-hood. Since Winkler's extended family was large, the agency's report was long, but all that he wanted to read about was visible on the first page. His grandmother, brother, mother, and father were dead, apparently victims of the First World War. He read just that first page, then tore up the report.

On board ship.

Whether or not Winkler's stories about his Austrian past were accurate, he always emphasized that the main event of his early life was arrival in the United States. It was clear to him that his real life commenced when he set foot on American soil, for the Atlantic crossing was a sloughing off of the past in hopes of attaining a new persona. The exact moment at which he asserted the identity by which he was ever after known occurred on Ellis Island when the immigration officer asked whether he wanted to change his name on entry to the United States. Catching up with his dreams, the boy John William Winkler replied, "I already have."

We do not know just when he arrived in New York, although the probabilities favor the fall of 1910. Neither do we know how long he spent traveling across the United States. He had ample funds, no responsibilities, and indulged in any whim or impulse that sparked his interest. Small wonder that he recalled this as a period when he was "free as a bird in the air." Remarkably, given the richness of Viennese culture and the imaginative excesses of his obsession with a dime novel America, he was never disappointed with the mundane truth of the New World—not even for one day, he always insisted. From the first New York cab driver—a *landsmann* who ran the meter to $10 for a one-block ride—Winkler overlooked the chicanery, the inconveniences, and the danger, and focused on the glory of an environment that more than fulfilled his fantasies. He found magic in such doubtful pastimes as walking dusty railroad tracks in the heat of the day while conversing with tramps and in feeding and housing a carnival Indian who then tried to rob him while he slept. He was determined to live and survive here, to make a million dollars and "show them all" back in Vienna—and also, of course, to find Buffalo Bill. And his enterprise was not defused when, upon reaching Nebraska, he discovered that the great showman was at that moment on tour in Europe. But his travels were by then progressing beyond the images of novels into an aimlessness that was eloquent with the questions . . . who am I and what will I become?

Winkler made his way west in fits and starts, lingering for a time in Chicago and Nebraska, where German-speaking communities offered him a sort of home base and instructed him, after a fashion, in the language and manners of America. For his part, he applied himself diligently to acquiring the customs of the common man, enduring, for example, several weeks of relentless nausea before he could properly

Postcard to Lena Wright
c.1911. Pencil

smoke cigars. And he eagerly drank in the language of the streets, relying on his extraordinary ear for the nuance of sound so that he quickly became conversant in American slang and could get along in English on his own. (Winkler would never lose his love for the common American idiom; even at age eighty-five, through the Viennese accent he never completely overcame, he would reach for an occasional "hell-bent-for-leather" or "son'a bitch.") Thus he avidly pursued his affinity with everyday life, trying to blend in, trying to find a way to experience it from inside. But such was his makeup that real integration was not a possibility. Having begun as a visitor, he would remain in essence an observer, a quality that would serve him well in his later career.

Winkler said that he left Nebraska abruptly to avoid a marriage to Lena Wright.[5] His friends in Douglas County wished him to marry locally so they would have him as a neighbor, and he played along, wooing Miss Wright by producing over forty pencil-drawn copies of American postcards, four of which survive thanks to the fond remembrance of their recipient. But he had not come to America to settle down, or so he believed at the time. He traveled to Salt Lake City, where he suddenly decided to work in a gold mine. Armed with a handgun, he headed for Bingham Canyon, renowned in those days as much for its lawlessness as for its gold. The locals didn't like him and he couldn't find work, so, still pursuing the elusive million dollars, he followed the advice of a Bingham Canyon denizen who told him that prospecting was easy in Phoenix because—can you hear it coming?—gold lay about aboveground. He immediately caught a train for Arizona, but en route changed course for California on account of the poetry of the name Los Angeles, which Winkler mentally pronounced in German as "Los-An-GAY-less." And in that sleepy little town, which offered no amusements, he very narrowly avoided the recognition that his American tour had run out of destinations. But spared by an advertisement for the "crookedest railroad in the world," the Mt. Tamalpais Railway, he probably signed up for the package tour at the Peck-Judah Company on South Spring Street, including passage up the coast of California and through the Golden Gate to Sausalito. There he made connection with the rail system to Tamalpais' crest and the uneventful guest house Tavern of Tamalpais, from which he descended through the fog for the local ferry to San Francisco.

Invigorated by his arrival in a real city—he probably hadn't seen one in over a year—the flagging adventure assumed new life. Winkler understood at once that he would spend some time in San Francisco, but he certainly did not know (as he headed for the Barbary Coast bordello that he mistook for a legitimate hotel) that his rambling search of self had ended. Though from his earliest days he had loved music and pageantry, there is no indication of a prior interest in fine art. Thus, on arrival in San Francisco he possessed no concept of the currents in the wider world of American culture, currents that were about to claim his special talents and bestow upon him the uniquely American identity fo: which he yearned.

———

1. "The first time I went to school was a sheer accident. I had walked down to the Ferry Building from the Nelsons, you see, and I was walking back home, just a leisurely walk, but always a cigar in my mouth. I walked on the side where the Fairmont Hotel is and there I read the sign on the other side; 'San Francisco Institute of Art.' The gates were open and I went in. I asked Miss Farrington, 'How long does it take to make lots of money cartooning?' I was going to show my folks that I could make millions because I had already read—you see I already read and spoke a little bit of English—that Charles Dana Gibson makes $100,000 a year, and I immediately translated that into crowns. I will show them, you know. She said, 'Well, sometimes a year, sometimes two years.' So I said to myself, 'I'll stay here.' And I stayed five years. I enrolled right away and I wasn't there three weeks when great art dawned on me, what it really is." Taped commentary, John Winkler, n.d., Winkler Archives, El Cerrito, Calif.

2. John Winkler enrolled as an "All-Day" student and apparently paid the entire tuition for academic year 1912–1913 on entry. "Personal Accounts," vol. 6, p. 90; Harry Mulford, comp., "Students of the California School of Design 1907–1915, from Tuition Fee Ledgers," 1980; and Tuition Fee Ledgers and Class Attendance Records, San Francisco Art Institute Archives, Anne Bremmer Library, San Francisco, Calif.

3. The only person who seriously attempted to identify the Austrian teenager later known to us as John William Winkler was Dr. John Whitten. From 1966 into 1977, Whitten conducted searches in the archives of Vienna, relying on the artist's remarks and hints including Winkler's characterization of his father as a "paper general" named Rudolf. Whitten searched army records only to discover that from 1900 to 1910 no less than fifteen generals Rudolf had been commissioned. But none of these had a "promising" last name. Later, Whitten went to the Schottenfeld *gymnasium* and asked if a boy named Johann Wilhelm Josef appeared on their rolls for the years 1908–1909.
    On other occasions, Whitten searched the voluminous *Gothaischen*

Genealogischen Taschenbucher (der Gotha) for any family with the configuration father Rudolf, mother Elisabeth, grandmother Veronika, and with two sons. Although some promising combinations appeared within the Lichtensteins—who had owned large estates in Landskron where Winkler said he had often visited his grandmother—and also among the Schwarzenbergs, no high-ranked family showed the correct pattern of names.

Based on Winkler's holographic fragment (see p. 3), the inquiry was reopened in 1986 by asking Whitten to search the records of the Schotten *gymnasium*, also in Vienna, and look for a sixteen-year-old who took a "leave" but never returned. Whitten replied that among ten sons of the upper nobility in attendance 1907–1909, no such student was listed, but the question remains unanswered for those boys of lesser rank.

No one who heard Winkler's stories about his boyhood during the twilight years of Franz Josef's reign ever doubted that he came out of the Austrian nobility, but for personal reasons John William Winkler did not want us to know who he was. Dr. John Whitten to Mary Millman, three letters, 1986; Whitten to Elizabeth Winkler, 1977; taped conversation among Whitten, E. Winkler, and John Aronovici, July 5, 1977, Winkler Archives.

4. As in many subsequent enthusiasms, Winkler was not alone in his fascination with the American wild west. The "Tramp Movement," still largely undocumented as a cultural phenomenon, affected especially the intelligentsia of much of middle and eastern Europe at the turn of the century. The movement spawned not only the dime novels, but dude ranch–type camps where would-be cowboys could sit at campfire with guitars and fire bullets into trees, as well as American country and western music traditions in such unlikely venues as, for example, Czechoslovakia. National Public Radio, Morning Edition, September 3, 1992: William Drummond's interviews with Miroslav Cerni and Yuri Weiss, Czech entertainment executives, recalling the Tramp Movement in Czechoslovakia.

5. Winkler's devoted friends, William B. and Ida Mae DuBois, located Lena Wright (then Helena Wright Campbell) in Aurora, Nebraska, and interviewed her in June of 1982. As a young woman she had lived in Giltner and initially knew Winkler as one of Joe Gannon's corn shuckers. She recalled his drawing portraits of local people. Alice and Ray Gannon, Joe Gannon's relatives, answered a letter Winkler wrote from Paris in 1922. They said, "Do you remember the card you glued Myra's baby picture on and drew flowers and butterflies around about? We have it yet, also the one of W.H. Taft. I don't know what Lena did with her pictures. It was surely a lucky day for you when you left Hamilton County, without Lena. She was never the girl for you. . . ." Alice and Ray Gannon to Winkler, October 26, 1922, Winkler Archives.

2. *He has been bitten by the etching bug* . . . Robert Harshe,
"The California Society of Etchers" in *Art in California,*
R.L. Bernier, San Francisco, 1916

J ust about the time that John Winkler was employing the bridges of
Chicago as a platform from which to perfect the New World art of
spitting Bull Durham—the year was 1910—a young woman named
Bertha E. Clausen Jaques convened a handful of etchers in a basement
room at the Art Institute of Chicago for the purpose of forming
the Chicago Society of Etchers, an association to be dedicated to
the promotion of etching as a fine art and to the mass marketing of the
etched image.

Etching had been "revived" in France in the 1850s and 1860s by an
art movement whose standard-bearer was a modern figure called the
"painter-etcher." Using "picturesque" rather than ideal or classical subject
matter, the painter-etcher's work was spontaneous, expressive, and
"autographic." In other words, the painter-etcher created *artistic* products
distinguishable from and superior to the purely illustrative images of
previous generations of European etchers.[1]

By the 1880s, partly as a consequence of proselytizing by French art
dealers, the revival had taken root in the upper echelons of the American
art community, and the New York Etching Club, essentially a collection
of fine painters, attempted to bring forth an indigenous movement of
painter-etchers. A number of excellent etchings were produced but this
first American revival, allied as it was with the French movement, did
not penetrate to the popular consciousness nor did it survive very long. It
seems significant that James McNeill Whistler, considered America's
premier painter-etcher, left the United States forever in 1855, published
his first etchings (*Douze eaux-fortes d'après nature,* referred to in English
as *The French Set*) in 1859 in Paris, directly under the influence of the

Bertha Jaques—"At my press" c.1897

French movement, and spent the remainder of his life primarily in England, where the British counterpart to the French movement grew up around Whistler and his colleague, Seymour Hayden.[2] Whistler's views about etching were publicized in American art periodicals and his works were exhibited in the United States, but American etching had no resident leader and by the turn of the century it was disorganized and somewhat adrift.

Thus Bertha Jaques referred to a lull of more than a generation when she noted that the new association "had existed potentially in several individuals who have been working in more or less solitary fashion for many years."[3] Jaques herself had come to the medium of etching in solitary fashion. Born in Covington, Ohio, in 1863, she did not take up printmaking until 1893, after she viewed the works of Whistler, Zorn, Cameron, and others at Chicago's World's Columbian Exposition. Gathering her earliest ideas from standard reference books on etching and very eclectic in her first materials—copper from kettle bottoms, discarded dentists' drills for needles—it was two full years before she produced a print that clearly showed she had gained the upper hand in the struggle with technique, yet she did not publicly show her etchings until 1903. Her devotion to etching deepened as she became imbued with the doctrine of the painter-etcher. By 1910 she had developed not only a purpose but also a plan.

The Chicago Society of Etchers, with Jaques as secretary (a post she would retain until 1937), held its first public exhibition in January of 1911. Success was immediate. The works of fifty-four etchers displayed at the Art Institute of Chicago were favorably reviewed in the March 1911 edition of *The International Studio*: "The first annual exhibition of this infant society was notable. Besides securing dignified recognition from official art circles, it excited much favorable comment from gallery frequenters. It received substantial returns financially. During the nineteen days of the display a large number of prints were purchased."[4]

The exhibition marked the beginning of more than two decades of success for the Society and, in a wider arena, the birth of the second revival of American etching. Bertha Jaques had structured the Society to benefit not only the twenty charter members, but etchers everywhere and even artists not yet won over to the medium, since she understood that the future of etching in the United States depended on finding and encouraging new talent.[5] Her central and most cherished goal was "to guide young etchers and instruct aspiring ones." At the same time she promoted numerous activities designed to awaken the American arts community to the beauties of the fine print, and carried the original work of individual artists to the doorsteps of the American purchasing public.

Despite organizational genius, the enterprise would have remained the property of the American artistic elite without the enthusiasm of the public at large. Fed by an evolving "etching craze," the Chicago Society of Etchers grew into an international organization that spawned print clubs (based on Jaques' excellent design) in key locations around the country. Bertha Jaques herself proved a masterful and indefatigable correspondent, always available to consult, advise, and encourage new organizations; through her energies young artists who might otherwise have ignored the etching medium were embraced and shepherded to prominence in the national arts community.[6]

The state of etching on the West Coast about 1910 was far more tenuous and fragmented than in the East.[7] Despite a respectable complement of promising young artists and the country's richest natural endowment of artistic subject matter, the "Pacific slope" arts community considered itself parochial—cut off from the main artistic currents of the nation. The graphic arts were wholly in the service of commercial enterprise, and etching, so little in evidence that the general public could not distinguish it from ink drawing, was literally unrecognized as a fine art. It is somewhat surprising, then, that San Francisco should have been so close on the heels of the establishment of the Chicago Society as to announce the formation of the California Society of Etchers in January of 1913.[8]

The California Society appears to have been the inspiration of four men: Robert B. Harshe, etcher and Stanford University art professor; Pedro J. Lemos, etcher and newly appointed professor of commercial reproduction at the San Francisco Institute of Art; Ralph Stackpole, sculptor; and Gottardo Piazzoni, painter. The Society was born at a dinner in December of 1912, for which Harshe said he paid the bill and was rewarded by election to the presidency.[9] Although there is no documentary evidence of the connection, it seems likely that the visit of notable American artist and patron Joseph Pennell to San Francisco in March of 1912, together with his December exhibition at the prestigious gallery of Vickery, Atkins & Torrey of the San Francisco municipal subjects he had etched that spring, gave impetus for the dinner and creation of the organization.[10] It may well have been that Pennell's San Francisco etchings caused Harshe and his friends to face the uncomfortable fact that the West would have almost nothing to show for itself in the way of printmaking at the Panama-Pacific International Exposition, then only two years away.

Bertha Jaques had demonstrated that an etchers' society could promote the cause of fine printmaking, but the California Society of Etchers was not to be a carbon copy. The task on the West Coast was much more demanding than picking up threads of the first revival of American etching. Lacking even a loose community of practitioners, the California group was constrained to bring forth etchers, etching, and an appreciative public. Nevertheless, the California Society of Etchers fairly burst upon the local scene with an exhibition in April of 1913, attacking all fronts with levity and not a little chaos. Later, the *San Francisco Chronicle* commentator, reviewing the more accomplished first annual exhibition in December, could not decide whether "an uplift or an uprising" was taking place.[11]

The Society was determined to make knowledgeable viewers out of the local populace, print purchasers and "refined" connoisseurs out of the common man with "limited means," and practicing etchers out of any artists who would listen. The major effort in the first year was publicity—two public exhibitions, lectures, an illustrated catalogue, a poster, and live public demonstrations of etching techniques. The tenor of these events may perhaps be gleaned from Harshe's description of the reaction of the San Francisco Sketch Club to a demonstration on their premises: "It was unanimously agreed by the throngs of clubwomen who gathered about the arena that an art which required such self-sacrifice, such immolation into unbelievable regions of dirt and ink and grime was indeed worthwhile. Solemnly and with conviction, I declare that this was the real beginning of interest in prints on the Pacific Coast."[12]

At least in its pre-Exposition years, the California Society was not so much an organization of etchers as a collection of artists established in other fields who wished to become printmakers. The initial membership was limited to resident Californians who had any previous experience with the etching technique and allied processes. To these painters and sculptors who were admittedly trying " 'prentice hands" on difficult media,[13] the Society imparted wholesale the doctrine of the painter-etcher. The hope was to engender a school of modern etching on the West Coast. Hill Tolerton, one of the Society's first five associate members and founder of The Print Rooms (which would become San Francisco's leading print gallery and headquarters for the Society after the Exposition) spoke for the Society when he said: "One of the peculiar charms of a properly executed etching is the fact that an artist is enabled in this manner to express in sure, swift lines the fleeting and transitory inspiration of the moment, and to give an interpretation of a given scene as it appears to him. Consequently you invariably see the scene through the artist's eyes. You see not only what he sees, but as he saw it when the mood that suggested the picture was dominant."[14] In short, etching was truly "autographic"—spontaneous, expressive, and personal. These qualities made etching the "essence of art," and in its ascendancy the California Society saw the elevation of all other art forms.

Due in part to the energies and good-humored opportunism of the founding members, and an early decision to admit nonresidents which brought notable artists to the fold,[15] the California Society had accomplished all of its early goals within three years of its formation. From its inception the Society had aimed for "worthy representation" in the fine arts exhibit of the Panama-Pacific International Exposition, scheduled to open in San Francisco in February of 1915. A good portion of the Society's success was due to the confluence of its own efforts with the growing enthusiasm for the arts engendered by the Exposition. Robert Harshe, perhaps by virtue of his presidency of the Society, was named organizer of the Exposition's print section and put together what was regarded then (and now) as the most important print exhibition in the United States up to that time.[16] Seven resident Society members exhibited there, and the Society's printmakers took three silver and two bronze medals.[17] Following this triumph, Pedro J. Lemos, the Society's first secretary, declared: "The 'wild and wooly west' is coming into its own again. California is buying etchings. Buying small prints, and without color. And there is no greater indication of the rise of art, and that California will become the art center of the West, than this fact."[18]

The California Society had succeeded in creating broad-based excitement about printmaking and a commitment among the local arts establishment to etching. By 1913 etching was so much in the air in San Francisco that it is not too great an exaggeration to suggest that John Winkler encountered it by the mere act of breathing.

1. Rona Schneider, "American Etching Revival: Its French Sources and Early Years," *American Art Journal* 14 (Autumn 1982): 40–65.

2. Allen Staley, introduction to *The Stamp of Whistler*, by Robert H. Getscher (Oberlin, Ohio: Allen Memorial Art Museum, 1974), pp. 3–5.

3. [Bertha E. Jaques], *Catalogue of an Exhibition of Works by American Etchers* (Chicago: Art Institute of Chicago, 1911).

4. Maude I. G. Oliver, "The Chicago Society of Etchers' First Exhibition," *International Studio* 42 (March 1911): iv–v.

5. "B.J. was the most important figure in the U.S. in connection with prints for the period from 1910 to 1935. For at least one year, and perhaps more, sales in the annual Chicago show exceeded ten thousand dollars, and this money was spread mostly among young and needy etchers. Or at least needy! I know of no one else who has done as much." Roi Partridge, Roi Partridge Papers, Book 4, Bancroft Library, Berkeley, Calif.

6. "Etching in America would never have reached such a height, as soon, if ever, if at the right moment it had not found the right person to encourage its growth and give it aid in word and deed. I feel sure that no one in the country has done so much for the development of art as Mrs. Jaques has done for etching." Howell C. Brown, "An Appreciation," *Print Society of California Newsletter* 10 (October–November 1931).

7. It was asserted that there were only 20 etchers in the entire West. S. Cheny, "Notable Western Etchers," *Sunset Magazine*, no. 21 (1908): 737–43.

8. "Etchers Form a State Organization. Many Local Artists Are Enrolled. Two Exhibitions a Year, With Demonstrations, Are Planned," *San Francisco Chronicle*, January 19, 1913.

9. Robert B. Harshe, "The California Society of Etchers," *Art in California* (1916; reprint ed., Irvine, Calif.: Westphal Publishing, 1988), pp. 116–120.

10. Raymond L. Wilson, "The Rise of Etching in American's Far West," *Print Quarterly* 2 (September 1985): 194–205.

11. "The California Society of Etchers is holding its first exhibit since organization at the galleries of Vickery, Atkins & Torrey on Sutter Street," *San Francisco Chronicle*, April 6, 1913; "Display of Etchings at the Sketch Club Opens for Fortnight," *San Francisco Chronicle*, December 7, 1913.

12. Harshe, p. 117.

13. ". . . many sculptors and painters are trying 'prentice hands on that which is said to be the most difficult of all, but with corresponding fascination. Those in authority state that nothing so shows the actual characteristics of an artist as does etching and that the required craftsmanship is so complex that any phase of success merits commendation." "Display of Etchings at the Sketch Club Opens for Fortnight," *San Francisco Chronicle*, December 7, 1913.

14. Hill Tolerton, "Etching and Etchers," *Art in California*, p. 121.

15. Prominent California members of the society included: Xavier Martinez, Joseph Raphael, Joseph Stanton, William Sparks, Armin Hansen, Frank Van Sloun, and Perham Nahl. When the society decided to admit nonresident artists, noted printmakers including Helen Hyde, Worth Ryder, Lee Randolph, Carl Oscar Borg, and Bertha Jaques also joined.

16. Wilson, "Rise of Etching"; Michael Williams, *A Brief Guide to the Palace of Fine Arts Panama Pacific International Exposition Post-Exposition Period* (San Francisco; San Francisco Art Association, 1915), p. 45.

17. California Society of Etchers members who exhibited at the Panama-Pacific were Armin C. Hansen, Robert B. Harshe, Pedro J. Lemos, Xavier Martinez, Perham W. Nahl, Roi Partridge, and Gottardo F. Piazzoni. Silver medalists were Clark Hobart, Perham Nahl, and Worth Ryder; bronze medalists were George T. Plowman and Helen Hyde; and honorable mentions went to Xavier Martinez and Pedro J. Lemos. *Illustrated Catalogue of Post-Exposition Exhibition* (San Francisco: San Francisco Art Association, 1916), p. 108.

18. Pedro J. Lemos, "California and Its Etchers, What They Mean to Each Other," *Art in California*, p. 113.

Winkler in class at SFIA by "Howard"
March 1914. Pastel on paper

3. *Winkler will surpass Whistler.* SFIA classmate on blackboard, 1915

Although John William Winkler (later John William Joseph Winkler) was adamant about the use of his full American name in the context of his artistic career, he proved unable to enforce such formality in less public realms. Evidently dissatisfied with the bland appellation "John," his friends at the San Francisco Institute of Art had by 1915 dubbed him "Wink," a name that use softened to "Winks" by the early 1930s. "John William Winkler" served as a title which he had both created and, through his etching, earned; but by a wide consensus in which he himself participated, for half a century the name "Winks" described the man.

While there is no particular reason to doubt Winks' oft-repeated assertion that he entered the San Francisco Institute of Art on pure impulse, it must be said that the transformation which followed was nothing short of miraculous. Winks enrolled as a near desperate self-orphaned European teenager more or less at the end of his fantasies, and in three short years emerged a full-blown American painter-etcher. That he entered SFIA aflame with the notion that cartooning would make him rich suggests both a lack of serious artistic intent and an ignorance of his own gifts. And yet he passed effortlessly from a freewheeling life devoted to self-gratification into a close-knit group with an authoritarian hierarchy structured around values and experiences that were entirely unknown to him. Winks himself said that entry into the Institute changed his life dramatically by offering to him the vision of great art, beside which cartooning quickly paled. The Institute's emphasis on drawing from life and constant sketching practice, a pedantic focus that was universal among American art schools of the time, may have prompted the revelation that he should draw what his eye took in and, further, that "greatness" resided in the skill with which he might express his personal impression of the world.

The Institute's policy was to place a new student who lacked formal training with a senior faculty member who would evaluate the student's potential at the end of the first year. Winks had the good fortune to come under the tutelage of Theodore Wores, a San Francisco portrait and landscape painter of international reputation, a member of the Institute's first class in 1874 who had served as dean in the difficult years after the 1906 earthquake. In 1912 Wores was nearing the end of his long tenure on the faculty. A soft-spoken, gentlemanly individual, he more than tolerated the impertinence of his eager student, permitting Winks to place an oversized easel at the head of the class, heedlessly blocking the view of other students. But Wores also delivered attentive and candid criticism, once remarking in class that a charcoal drawing Winks had belabored for more than a week had come to resemble a sack of coal. Conservative in his views as in his work, Wores venerated the great masters of painting and often held their opinions and their achievements up to the class for emulation. It was certainly Wores who first introduced Winks to the glories of great art and moved him to replace his desire to unseat cartoonist Charles Dana Gibson with the aspiration to become a great painter.

After Wores left the Institute, Winks attached himself to Frank Van Sloun, a painter and a devoted educator who continued to nourish Winks' ambitions. And Winks quickly distinguished himself as a talented painter within the small circle of the Institute, for within two years he was one of four day students awarded a tuition-free honorary scholarship,[1] an award based on the merit of his work in class, which was exclusively drawing and oil painting. (Winks continued to paint seriously until 1921, when he left for Paris with his canvases rolled carelessly one on top of the other for transport. On arrival in France he discovered that they had melted together; deeply discouraged by the loss of eight years' work, he abandoned oil painting forever.)

It might have been predictable that success within the formal structure of the Institute, even rapid success, would not entirely satisfy Winks. His soaring ambitions and his inability to resist things popular, colorful, and energetic make it impossible to imagine that Winks could have remained untouched by the etching craze at that very moment rampant in the microcosm of the Institute. Pedro J. Lemos became an instructor there in the fall of 1912 and introduced etching to the curriculum, albeit with a commercial link, in a course entitled "Etching and Process Reproduction."[2] The rowdy California Society of Etchers conducted regular meetings on the premises of the Institute, starting in 1913, and attracted conservative faculty such as John A. Stanton and newcomers like Van Sloun. In March of 1914 the Institute hosted a Chicago Society of Etchers "rotary" (traveling) show, making available to students and the public the best contemporary work of the eastern etching movement, and emphasizing that etching was a national as well as a local and regional artistic cause. Then in the fall of 1914, "Etching, Theory and Practice" as taught by Lemos emerged as a separate course, and an etching prize appeared for the first time at the Institute in academic year 1914–1915. And finally, some portion of the frenzied preparation for the Panama-Pacific print exhibition must have been carried out in Lemos' classroom, although the Institute did not acquire its own etching press until 1915.

At the height of his etching career, Winks often told the press that he started to etch in 1915. But judging from the handful of student etchings that escaped Winks' despairing raids on his own work, and reasoning from his student career at SFIA, Winks probably started to etch in early 1913, indeed within a few months of his enrollment. The truth was, he could never say exactly when he started because he had picked up the needle in private—as a hobby, he said—and really had no idea of what was to come. In other words, there was no reason at all to mark the event.

Winks probably acquired his first ideas about etching technique from the live demonstrations staged by the California Society of Etchers in 1913, and with them the doctrine of the painter-etcher. Though Winks liked to describe himself as completely self-taught, even the earliest glimpses of his initial experiments with the medium make it clear that he had assimilated the entire painter-etcher persona. He made his plates *plein air*, spontaneously recording his impressions of the scene. Like other American etchers before him, his first materials were improvised—some discarded halftone plates from a *San Francisco Chronicle* trash bin for copper or zinc, and a laundry mangle in place of an etching press.[3] His subject matter was natural, available, and urban (it would be some years before he would admit that he scanned for the "picturesque" in his

Building City Hall 1914

environment), and he etched just where he practiced with his sketchbook —on the wharves, in the park, and in Chinatown,[4] though his earliest views of that intriguing quarter reveal Winks as an outsider, little more than a passerby. What interested him were vistas of the city, and to satisfy him the vistas needed to portray San Francisco's marine setting. He began to experiment with perspectives calculated to draw the viewer ever farther down bustling streets to the ocean or the bay. His initial style was a simple application of his pencil drawing methods to a grounded plate, another confirmation that his earliest notion was the direct rendition of his personal impression.

Winks probably etched on his own for about a year before he realized he was on to something. As the etching craze intensified he became more concerned with technique, and etching grew from a pastime to a serious artistic endeavor. In March of 1914, when the Chicago Society of Etchers rotary show was hanging at the Institute, Winks undertook a significant challenge: standing across the street and cradling a grounded zinc plate in his raised left arm, he needled the construction of the new City Hall just as the dome was taking shape. He worked on a larger plate than he had used before and thoughtfully composed the scene, relying exclusively on line to create all tonal effects. Later, at home, to correct the directional orientation of the building (an image needled on the plate exactly as observed creates a reversed image when printed), he transferred the composition to another plate and improved the foreground figures. These plates, *Building City Hall*,[5] mark the beginning of a distinctive etching style. The results must have pleased him, but we do not know whether he showed the prints to anyone at the time.

Still officially committed to painting, Winks was nearing the end of his fourth semester at the Institute. His classwork was highly regarded and he was about to receive the tuition-free scholarship. Surviving records do not reveal whether he attended the summer session (the first offered by the SFIA since the earthquake), but he doubtless continued etching that summer, and perhaps with some inkling of an identity that would shape his life he enrolled in Lemos' "Etching, Theory and Practice" class in the fall. In doing so, Winks quickly discovered that in his private experimentation he had evolved a personal etching technique that placed him at variance with the views of his instructor, who was also acting director of the school for that year. Though Winks never alienated Lemos (who assisted Winks in many ways, including sponsoring him for membership in the San Francisco Art Association in 1916), he

Post Street 1914

also never once acknowledged Lemos' assistance or influence and later disavowed the work he produced under Lemos' direction. (*Post Street*, the single surviving print that unquestionably came out of Lemos' class, carries Winks' penciled protest on the back . . . "told to leave the ink on!" He had apparently followed Lemos' instructions in the use of *retroussage*—leaving traces of ink on the unbitten portions of the plate to create tones or shadows in the print. But Winks wanted no part of that approach. He would rely instead on the purest of technique, creating his effects with bitten lines of infinite subtlety. Winks' single-minded reliance on line would become the hallmark of his mature style and his mastery of line the quality that, more than any other, made him an etcher's etcher.)

In his own style then, and most likely on his own time, in 1914–1915 Winks created a collection of San Francisco scenes including *Library Site, Hall of Records,* and *Stockton Street Tunnel,* which formed the nucleus of what might be called his first portfolio. Lighthearted in spirit, these straightforward views convey the young observer's pleasure with an urban landscape which excited him. As etchings, they are consistent with his earlier experiments. They are also unmistakably the work of a modern painter-etcher. The blustery breezes and simple charm of *Library Site,* for example, speak directly of Winks' delightful personal impression.

Meanwhile, at the Panama-Pacific's splendid exhibition of February 1915, Winks viewed for the first time the etched works of Whistler. Winks acknowledged that he was profoundly affected by them, but grumbled all his life against the frequent assertion of critics that his own work was derivative of Whistler's, and eventually backed himself into the corner of denying *any* Whistlerian influence, which was disingenuous at best. Considering how thoroughly his early artistic beliefs were molded by the environment of the San Francisco arts community, which venerated Whistler as the greatest American etcher and, second only to Rembrandt, the greatest etcher in the world, it is entirely likely that Winks saw in Whistler's work the highest expression of the very ideas that by now he considered his own. At the very least Whistler's work provided him with a sense of direction and possibly also delivered a challenge—could he *exceed* the work of the American master?

———————

The small group of San Francisco etchings stunned and excited Winks' colleagues and instructors at the Institute. By the end of the 1914–1915

Ferry Building and Post Office 1915

Windmill and Merry-Go-Round at Ocean Beach c.1914–1915

academic year he had emerged as the most promising young etcher on the local horizon, the artist for whom all San Francisco had been searching prior to the Panama-Pacific. His etchings outshone his paintings and pen-and-ink drawings at the SFIA student exhibition in May of 1915, earning him the Institute's first etching prize and, subsequently, the school's highest honor—a life scholarship.[6] His classmates paid him the lofty, if unnecessary, compliment of pilfering his works from his locker even though Winks freely gave them away to anyone who asked.[7] And someone wrote on a classroom blackboard: "Winkler will surpass Whistler."

---

1. Honorary scholarships for day class students (1914–1915) were awarded to John W. Winkler, Emma V. Wirtz, Elizabeth Daniels, and Elvida C. Antonovich. The awards were announced at the student reception of the SFIA annual exhibition on May 15, 1915. "Minutes, College Committee, Original Drafts, 1914–1915," San Francisco Art Institute Archives, Anne Bremmer Library, San Francisco, Calif.

2. Pedro J. Lemos attended SFIA in 1900. In 1911 he filled in for Charles Frank Ingerson by conducting the Decorative Design and Process Work class while Ingerson was abroad. Lemos became a faculty member in 1912, acting director of the 1914 summer school, acting director of the Institute in the fall of 1914, and director in 1915. During his tenure at SFIA he oversaw the modernization of the curriculum, adding to the old nucleus of painting, drawing and sculpture the new "applied" arts: illustration, decorative and commercial design, mural painting, interior decoration, etching, pottery, and handicrafts. Lemos was also instrumental in reconciling the Institute with the alienated local arts community, for which Maynard Dixon and Francis McComas were spokesmen, by including in the Institute's annual spring exhibition the works of local artists and former students. "Institute of Art on Eve of Renaissance," *San Francisco Chronicle*, August 13, 1914.

3. Or so he told Bertha Jaques, who published the information in the Chicago Society of Etchers' broadside that accompanied *Kong Tong & Co.*, the 1919 members' plate. *Ninth Publication of the Chicago Society of Etchers* (Chicago: Chicago Society of Etchers, 1919): Winkler Archives.

4. *End of Embarcadero, Windmill in Golden Gate Park*, and *Hang Far Lo.*

5. *Building City Hall* had some currency in the post-Exposition era in San Francisco. It was certainly exhibited at the SFIA student exhibition in May

of 1915 and probably shown at the California Society of Etchers fourth annual exhibition as well as the San Francisco Art Association's First Exhibition of Painting and Sculpture later that year. However, Winkler did not regard it as suitable work for it was not shown after 1916 and it does not appear in his San Francisco portfolio of the late 1910s and 1920s. Neither is it included in the *catalogue raisonné* published by *The Print Connoisseur* in 1924. *Building City Hall* was shown at the Walton Gallery (San Francisco) in 1974 and has been included among his etched works since then.

6.   Anna C. Winchell, "Art and Artists," *San Francisco Chronicle*, May 23, 1915.

7.   To this trait we owe the survival of a number of Winkler's student works, including *Fisherman's Retreat* which he gave to his classmate Douglas Grant in the spring of 1915. Mr. Grant preserved the etching and kindly provided it for reproduction in this publication.

Fisherman's Retreat 1915

End of the Embarcadero c.1913

Windmill in Golden Gate Park 1913

Market and Kearny Streets 1915

Hall of Records c.1915–1918

Russian Hill 1916

4. *Collectors who do not own some of his early Chinese subjects will miss the work that will probably always distinguish Mr. Winkler.* Christian Science Monitor, *November 29, 1920*

The years between the etching prize at SFIA (1915) and Winks' first showing of "three little prints" to the national arts community, at the American Institute of Graphic Arts' exhibition of "Etchings by Contemporary American Artists" in March of 1917,[1] are somewhat obscure, partly because Winks was still evolving as an etcher and hadn't really settled into his calling and partly because his etchings were not yet generating income. By mid-1915 he had finally run out of his grandmother's money and faced the stark alternatives of work or starvation. Although Winks once referred to his impoverishment as "the penalty for not going home," it does not appear that he even considered contacting Vienna for a further advance. So he needed to earn a living by wage labor, a condition entirely foreign to his cast of mind, a condition into which, except for the brief period between the Institute and substantial income from his etching, he never again lapsed. (He had flirted with work on his way across country, hiring himself out in Nebraska as a cornhusker in order to test the idea that the elusive million dollars might be garnered manually. But Winks' cornhusking career lasted all of one day because, remunerative or not, continually stripping ears of corn caused his wrists to swell so badly that he could not use his hands.)

In dire straits then, Winks turned to the Institute for help. SFIA had a long-standing and well-announced policy of assisting needy students find employment, and apparently was able to dole out San Francisco street jobs. And so it was that Winks became a gas lamplighter, a position which he greatly enjoyed and with which he identified to the degree that he listed himself in the *City Directory* for 1916 as "Lamplighter." The pay was two $20 gold pieces per month, an income that required spartan economies compared with his previous style, but the duties were light and did not interfere with daytime pursuits. Each lamplighter had an assigned route and was expected to keep the mantles in good condition, ignite the lights in the early evening, and return later to douse them. Winks later said the route took him a little less than an hour and that he was an indifferent worker, prone to neglecting not just single lamps but entire blocks. However, the company liked him and tended to overlook his shortcomings, and Winks, who always enjoyed being on the streets, made friends with the local constabulary who would remind him of lights he had forgotten. Lamplighting suited him so well that he kept the job until 1918.

There was nothing notable about Winks' last official year at the San Francisco Institute of Art. On tuition-free life scholarship, he enrolled in the fall of 1915 in Stanton's portrait class and Van Sloun's men's life drawing class, but from about November Winks distinguished himself primarily by persistent absence. Van Sloun benignly noted on the attendance sheet that Winks had been assigned to "outdoor sketching," but Stanton dropped him.[2] Spring semester found him enrolled in Van Sloun's life class again, which Winks had totally abandoned in March. This behavior did not signal disinterest; rather, by 1916 Winks was a student in name only, since with regard to his work and his personal presence as an artist he had already become an equal with his teachers.

Despite his youth (Winks was twenty-one at most in 1915) and despite a mere two and a half years' experience with the etching medium, in the last half of 1915 Winks assumed the status and the trappings of a professional painter-etcher. Shortly after the SFIA etching prize and apparently on the strength of the etchings he had produced to win it, Winks gained membership in the California Society of Etchers,[3] showing *Library Site* and *Building City Hall* at the Society's annual exhibition,[4] probably held in December of 1915. But a stronger indication of Winks' place in the San Francisco arts community of that year was his participation in the First Exhibition of Painting and Sculpture at the Golden Gate Park Memorial Museum, put on as a post-Exposition event by the San Francisco Art Association and featuring the work of every imaginable northern California artist of distinction.[5] In addition to the canvases of Theodore Wores, Arthur F. Matthews, Thomas Hill, Maynard Dixon, and Carl Oscar Borg, to name just a few, the exhibit included three entries of "art prints," as if to say that no modern exhibit would be complete without such media. Helen Hyde, a close friend of Bertha Jaques and internationally famous for her oriental prints, showed three works, Pedro Lemos showed two etchings and a watercolor, and John Winkler showed a collection of etchings entitled *Views of San Francisco*. Though not individually listed, these etchings must have been substantially identical with the works that had earned him the SFIA prize.

Though Winks was forging a reputation as San Francisco's own painter-etcher, he didn't stray far from the Institute. The summer of 1916 found John Winkler, not Pedro Lemos, teaching a course entitled "Etching and Pen and Ink Drawing," no doubt a welcome source of added revenue and also compatible with his lamplighting duties. Described in the catalogue as a "Member of the California Society of Etchers, exhibiting his work in several exhibitions," Winks offered the student "a thorough knowledge of his subject."[6] Though he never mentioned his teaching activities in later years, he must have discharged his duties creditably, because about a year later Van Sloun made Winks the functioning assistant director of the Van Sloun school, conducted in his studio at Ninth and Market streets. A short-lived offshoot of SFIA, the school was devoted exclusively to instruction in drawing and painting. According to Louis Siegrist (whom Van Sloun had personally wooed away from SFIA), Winks regularly managed the day-to-day instruction in place of Van Sloun, who was frequently absent on painting and mural assignments.[7]

But in Winks' lamplighting years, the California Society of Etchers, the exhibitions, and the teaching were all incidental to his main passion. The earliest clue to this is found in the SFIA summer school catalogue for 1916 in the reproduction of Winks' etching *Dark Alley*, the first known publication of any image from Chinatown. Taken together with the five additional Chinatown etchings Winks submitted for the San Francisco Art Association's 1916 annual exhibition,[8] *Dark Alley* shows not only quantum leaps in style and mastery but more importantly that Winks had found what would be the dominant subject matter of his life as an etcher.

His long and affectionate involvement with San Francisco's Chinese quarter was the happiest byproduct of the lamplighting job, for his route—in the vicinity of the Fairmont Hotel—took him just above DuPont Street and the heart of the district. Winks' irrepressible curiosity and imagination did the rest. Intensely fascinated with a community every bit as exotic as the East Indies fantasies of his childhood, Winks became a regular in Chinatown, by his own account spending every spare

Printed on the first paper made in the United States Single impression W

Winkler

weekday moment and every Saturday and Sunday there for about seven years. He came to know its public life in intimate detail and, although never admitted to its inner workings, was apparently accepted by the Chinese as a harmless curiosity. As observer and *plein air* etcher, Winks himself became part of the color of the place, a fact he acknowledged many years later by etching his own likeness among the crowds of Waverly Place in *Busy Day in Chinatown.*

Winks once said that in Chinatown he had "struck a gold mine," by which he certainly meant that his career was built on the plates that originated there. And if he had thought in such terms, he might also have said that in no other period of his life as an etcher did he produce so naturally and so prolifically. By 1918 he had made thirty-seven plates of Chinatown subjects and by 1921, when he left for Paris, he had created at least twice as many more. In the early 1920s he re-etched a number of them, issuing the new versions and recalling, or ordering the destruction of, old prints where possible. But a large number of Chinatown plates were never issued in the 1920s. Winks transported them to Paris where he worked on a few, and finally brought them back to San Francisco where he perfected and issued them over the remainder of his life. His experience in Chinatown was so profound and the visual imagery so rich that it sustained him as an artist long after he declined to visit the quarter because "it had completely changed."

The forty prints that earned him accolades in his early career (sometimes called "the Chinatown set") were almost entirely from plates he had created directly on the site. They spoke exclusively of Chinatown's streets—the architecture, the commerce, and all manner of life from surging crowds to reclusive individuals. Winks' unique relation to Chinatown allowed him to say as much with the fleeting interaction between a tortoise and a man trimming cabbage as he could with the crowded roadway and intricate facades of Waverly Place. He somehow put into the copper of every plate the deep respect, the gentle comprehension, and the great excitement he felt when he was in the quarter. In the highest painter-etcher tradition these plates bear Winks' most personal "autograph."

Even earliest viewers—connoisseurs and critics ever watchful for the emergence of the American painter-etcher—saw all this and more. They recognized a "remarkable talent," an artist "with a variety in the uses of the etched line that one finds only in the great etchers," a stylist whose subject matter was "handled with a delicacy and finesse such as are

Dark Alley 1916

the last desire of the etcher's art." Too frequently perhaps for Winks, they also saw the direct influence of Whistler, for the earliest commentary struck the oft-repeated chord that Winks' method approached "more nearly that of Whistler than do those of any other American etcher." And early on a few saw Rembrandt, a compliment so lofty that Winks could not afford to disdain it and which contained a hint of the factor common to the admiration of the diverse critics of his Chinatown studies. Beyond the intriguing subject matter, the "beautiful sincerity" of presentation, and the stunning virtuosity of line, the critics universally saw in Winks' plates etching itself in its purest form. In 1920, Frank W. Benson was first to point out that the subject matter was almost beside the point: "Such etching as Mr. Winkler's depends little on the motives [motifs] etched; it is a medium of expression so admirably used that it is hard to see how it could be bettered."[9] The level of such praise must have seemed to Winks a long distance indeed from the streets of Chinatown, but the fact remained that his Chinatown plates represented a newfound and exuberant achievement unique to him. With unusual foresight the commentator for the *Christian Science Monitor* offered this advice to his readers in November of 1920: "Collectors who do not own some of his early Chinese subjects will miss the work that will probably always distinguish Mr. Winkler."[10]

---

1.   *At Leisure, Freighting*, and *Irmgard*. Other etchers represented in this exhibition included: John Taylor Arms, Frank W. Benson, Benjamin C. Brown, Howell C. Brown, Ernest Haskell, Bertha E. Jaques, Pedro J. Lemos, Gertrude Partington, Roi Partridge, and Joseph Pennell. *An Exhibition of Etchings by Contemporary American Artists* (New York: American Institute of Graphic Arts, 1917).

2.   "Attendance Reports 1915–1916," San Francisco Art Institute Archives, Anne Bremmer Library, San Francisco, Calif.

3.   Winkler liked to say that he was a charter member of the California Society of Etchers. While this is not literally true, he was admitted to membership early in the history of the organization. The copy of the society's July 1915 *Constitution and By-Laws* preserved by the Bancroft Library includes a printed membership list at the end of which "John Winkler S.F. Inst. of Art" has been added in pen, apparently to record his admission just after the list went to the printer.

4. The show included fifty-one etchings, six lithographs, and nineteen color prints of various types. Other exhibiting etchers included Carl Oscar Borg, Armin Hansen, Roi Partridge, and Bertha Jaques. *Fourth Annual Exhibition* (San Francisco: California Society of Etchers, 1915).

5. Other exhibitors included Julian Rix, Charles Rollo Peters, Clarkson Dye, G. Cadenasso, Xavier Martinez, G. Piazzoni, Will Sparks, Armin Hansen, F. Burgdorff, Frank Van Sloun, William Silva, Hanson Puthuff, [Alexis Matthew] Podchernikoff, A. W. Best, Gordon Coutts, William F. Jackson, Charles Dorman Robinson, Thadeus Welch, William Keith, Jules Pages, Louise M. Carpenter, Harry Cassie Best, Percy Gray, Mary de Neale Morgan, Arthur Beckwith, Bertha Stringer Lee, and Christian Jorgensen. *First Exhibition of Painting and Sculpture* (San Francisco: Golden Gate Park Memorial Museum, n.d.).

6. *Art Summer Session* (San Francisco: San Francisco Institute of Art, 1916).

7. "Van Sloun was so busy doing murals that he had John Winkler more or less run the whole school. All they had was a life class there and Winkler taught it. But I never saw him etch. He must have done that somewhere else. Winkler was quite well thought of as a painter. He liked to paint large canvases. I watched him paint quite a bit in class." Taped interview with Louis Siegrist by Mary Millman, December 1985.

8. Winkler submitted the following titles for the 1916 San Francisco Art Association annual exhibition: *Black Alley—Chinatown, Sailing Boat Irmgard, Russian Hill, Freight in Chinatown, At Leisure Chinatown, Chinatown, The Tunnel,* and *Up Hill Chinatown.* Exhibition application, Winkler Archives.

9. Frank W. Benson, foreword to *An Exhibition and Private Sale of Etchings by John W. Winkler* (Boston: Doll & Richards, 1920): Doll & Richards Exhibition Catalogs 1912–1941, roll NDR1, frames 362–363, Archives of American Art, Smithsonian Institution.

10. "When a New Star Appears," *Christian Science Monitor,* November 29, 1920.

Busy Day in Chinatown c.1917–1920

Corner Fruitstand 1918

Noon Rest 1918

5. *Our Chinatown held me spellbound as long as I stayed in San Francisco.* Winkler to a Miss Watson, 1970

Winks' discovery of Chinatown and its "inexhaustible variety of enticing subject matter"[1] deepened his personal commitment to etching. Just to be close to the Chinese quarter, in mid-1916 he took up furnished rooms at the Glencliff (679 Pine Street) with his friend Leon Abrams,[2] then a young photographer for the *San Francisco Chronicle.* The pair observed an eccentric schedule, ostensibly dictated by photographic and lamplighting duties but in truth calculated to avoid the landlady's inquiries about the rent. When slipping out of the Glencliff at six a.m. no longer worked, they rose earlier, sometimes at three, and never returned before ten at night when they knew Mrs. Zwicker would be asleep.

In those days, Winks' habit of biting the Chinatown plates late into the night was as much a symptom of his financial condition as it was of the intensity with which he worked. He had abandoned the standard practice of submerging his plates in an acid bath, and turned to Whistler's method of gently working the acid over small sections to achieve diversity in the quality of the etched line. He also insisted on printing his own plates,[3] for he was anxious to govern personally all aspects of the process to insure the integrity of the expression in each image. When he pulled the proofs his confidence was such that he was eager to get the images before the public, and by the end of 1916 he had issued and exhibited in San Francisco at least six Chinatown scenes. With these and more recent work, in early 1917 he made his first submission to a national exhibition.

Winks never indicated what caused him to send his work to the American Institute of Graphic Arts in New York for its March exhibition of "good honest painter-etchings," selected from "a veritable revival of etching in this country."[4] He must have been warmly encouraged to do so by his colleagues in the California Society of Etchers (a number of whom had tried their hand in Chinatown but with less inspired results), who apparently regarded this one-time comprehensive national exhibition as a cut above the annual shows of the print clubs. Of the 102 contemporary American etchers presented in the New York show, nineteen were nonresident and four were resident members of the California Society.[5] Winks had the largest representation among the San Franciscan printmakers with three etchings: *At Leisure* and *Freighting* from Chinatown, and *Irmgard* from San Francisco's waterfront. Along with the works of other young etchers Winks' prints compared favorably with those of established artists such as Ernest D. Roth and Frank W. Benson, although his first exposure to the national arts community produced no miracles. But he had staked out a modest niche in the national panorama, more or less an extension of his prominence in San Francisco circles.

By 1917 the European war had invaded everyone's daily consciousness, casting long shadows of fear and suspicion across American society. Considering the high pitch of anti-German hysteria then sweeping the West Coast, one wonders if Winks' practice of pinning lists of English words to a clothesline strung up in his room at the Glencliff was motivated by a desire to subdue his telltale accent, and as the local newspapers headlined the war he could not have been indifferent to the grave threat to his high-ranking family in Austria. But by now thoroughly American in sentiment and allegiance, Winks was the 331st person to register at his local draft board on Sansome Street, and for a time he was eager to be called, imagining the war as another grand adventure. Fate ultimately spared him, for which he had the good sense to be grateful in retrospect, but so many of his fellow artists enlisted that the Van Sloun school had to close its doors toward the end of the year for want of male students.

Despite the disturbance and gloom, in 1917 Winks achieved a quality of artistic result that can only be described as mastery, and a level of productivity that he would sustain for nearly a decade to come. Perhaps inevitably, new recognitions about etching accompanied this achievement: Winks came to understand that the perfected painter-etcher product proceeded from the marriage of impulse and technique, the surge of feeling literally selecting its own form of expression. (Winks remarked in 1918 that nearly all his earlier plates had been "the result of inspirational moments, scratched from nature without being conscious of technique," while the more recent ones were "preconceived, coldly and deliberately worked out." By applying the full force of his intellect to his work, Winks saw anew "the great possibilities that art has in store for those who can, in moments of inspiration, turn to their storehouse of technical resources and unconsciously take from it whatever the subject requires."[6] And so, high-mindedly refusing various commercial art assignments from Van Sloun and others, including the chance to etch a picture of someone's house for a $10 fee, he pursued his old haunts with heightened awareness of his mission as a painter-etcher.

In Chinatown he apparently shifted focus from the architectural vistas and the street trade to the shopkeepers and the sidestreet merchants, creating between late 1916 and early 1918 a remarkable subset of the Chinatown work comprised of at least six major plates: *Chowseller, Gingershop, The Delicatessen Maker, Oriental Quarter, Corner Fruitstand,* and *Quiet Corner.* No longer necessarily satisfied with the image as he needled it on the scene, Winks now took the *plein air* plate back to the Glencliff where he etched and re-etched until he produced an answer to his exacting requirements for technical presentation and self-expression. In some cases, most notably *The Delicatessen Maker* (perhaps his single most admired work, issued in final form from Paris in 1923), this process of refinement took years to complete, leaving in its wake a succession of "old" plates and superseded prints. In 1917, however, Winks was content with the rigorous application of his newly acquired judgment. Thus, in the new waterfront subject matter developed in 1917, he can be observed unconsciously taking from his technical storehouse "whatever the subject required." Building on the wharfside perspective he experimented with in the plate *Irmgard,* from the edge of San Francisco's China Basin he needled one of his most famous images, erroneously titled from the day of its creation *Mission Street Wharf.* Interestingly, this plate was perfectly executed in its *plein air* version and resisted his later efforts to improve it. He made it larger, smaller, and even took a "detail" from its center. Yet the most he could ever bring himself to alter was the number of gulls in the air.

———————————

Prevailing sentiment in the California Society of Etchers with respect to the locus of picturesque subject matter came to favor the remote Oakland

Gingershop 1917

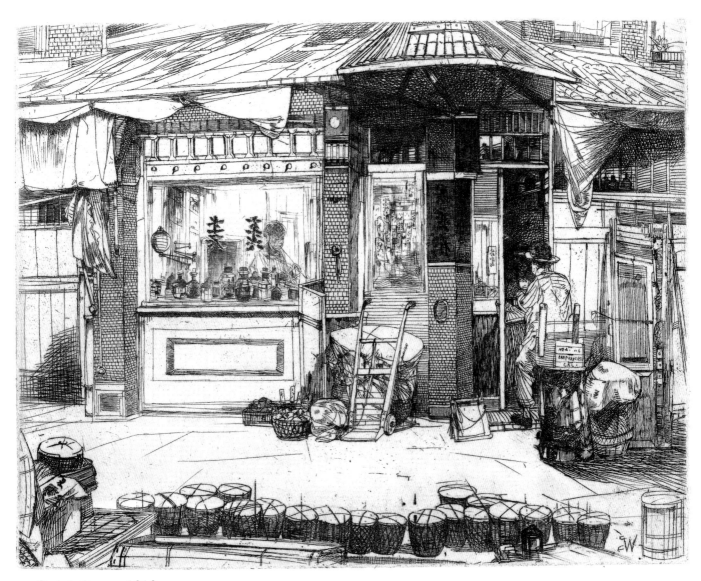

Quiet Corner 1918

The Delicatessen Maker 1917

Chowseller 1916

estuary over San Francisco's familiar cluttered docks. So Winks began to ferry over to Alameda in search of new vistas to etch. He was thrilled to discover there the rotting ships of the old hay schooner fleet[7] and the idle hours of ghostly exploration they provided, and from time to time, inspired by some particular view, he etched according to his new insights, early on producing two "cold" and "deliberate" exercises in composition, *On the Mud Flats* and *View of Oakland*. Though our modern eye is seldom asked to supply visual substance that is actually absent from an image, the educated viewer of Winks' day found high excitement in the ability of bare lines to call forth an entire visual panorama. In *View of Oakland* and subsequent etchings, especially in the waterfront series, Winks' use of line was so sparse as to be courageous in its transformation of blank paper into shimmering water. With seemingly effortless economy, he led the eye directly to the quiet expanse and stepped aside in absolute confidence that light and air, and even color, would shortly present themselves. The evocative Oakland estuary plates— the proving ground for Winks' experiments with technique—would also be an important addition to his carefully selected repertoire of subjects.

---

1. "Our Chinatown held me spellbound as long as I stayed in San Francisco. Nowhere could I find such an inexhaustible variety of enticing subject matter. As soon as school was out I was on its streets with a plate in my hand that had not a line on it, standing by the hour working until I reached what I considered an adequate rendering of the scene before me." Winkler to a Miss Watson, September 23, 1970, Winkler Archives.

2. According to Winkler, Leon "Lee" Abrams was his oldest friend. Born in Leavenworth, Kansas, July 28, 1892, Abrams came to San Francisco in 1910. He worked for the *Chronicle* until he became an army pilot in World War I. He moved to Paris in the early 1920s and he and Winkler saw much of each other there. Abrams directed Sarah Bernhardt in a motion picture during his stay in France. Later he moved to New York, where his play "Heat Lightning" was produced on Broadway and subsequently made into a movie. He went on to become a writer and film executive with Metro-Goldwyn-Mayer and Universal Studios. He died July 5, 1977, in Moraga, California. Winkler visited him often in his old age. Obituary, *San Francisco Chronicle*, July 7, 1977.

3. It is not precisely known where Winkler printed in these years. The new etching press at SFIA was available to him at least through the summer of 1916.

East Oakland c.1919

The Print Rooms had an etching press on the premises, perhaps the property of the California Society of Etchers for which the gallery served as headquarters. Snapshots of Winkler's apartment at 728 Pine Street show a small etching press in the living room.

4.   W.H. deB. Nelson, foreword to *An Exhibition of Etchings by Contemporary American Artists* (New York: The American Institute of Graphic Arts, 1917), pp. 7–8.

5.   Pedro J. Lemos was represented by two aquatints and Lee F. Randolph by a drypoint. Gertrude Partington showed two etchings, *Chinatown* and *On Telegraph Hill.* Of the seventy-eight charter members of the California Society— i.e., members at the time of publication of the constitution and by-laws in July, 1915—thirty were resident in the Bay Area.

6.   [Bertha E. Jaques], *Ninth Publication of the Chicago Society of Etchers* (Chicago: Chicago Society of Etchers, 1919): Winkler Archives.

7.   "... went to Sausalito to see the three-masted sailing ship, *Rose*-or-something-of-the-Pacific. Stayed on it for several hours. Captains Gow, Pearson, and Robinson, all former masters of sailing ships, on board. Every one of them a character out of a book. The present owner, Mrs. Kininger, also on board. The vessel was her home for twenty years when she sailed with her husband, the captain. He has passed on to better seas. When I asked if the ship was not a former whaler [hay schooner], I was told it was, and that it was the *Star of Alaska.* The answer nearly knocked me overboard. As a young student I went often to the estuary in Oakland where, for years, the old ships were rotting in the water, crowded together like chickens in a coup. It was plenty of fun to board them and roam about for hours, instead of working. I remember best the *Star of Alaska* because I spent more time on it than the others. If someone had told me that forty years later I would again set food on board...! About 1916 to 1954!" Winkler diary entry, March 28, 1954, Winkler Archives.

View of Oakland c.1916

Alameda c.1919

Abandoned Alaska Fleet [*Rickety Pier*] c.1920

Shipping 1919

Mission Street Wharf 1918

Nora Crowe Winkler at
728 Pine Street, c.1918–1919

6. *His style is marked by a beautiful brevity and reticence.*
W.H. Downes, Boston *Evening Transcript*, November 11, 1920

With the new Chinatown plates, the waterfront images, and his older San Francisco views, to which he had added several creditable scenes after he left the Institute, Winks possessed a portfolio of over forty etchings, a figure he would double in the next three years. He had already produced some of his most compelling work, and in the full swing of his creative years he was well prepared for what was on the horizon.

As with so many other events in his early life, the beginning of Winks' acquaintance with Bertha Jaques was obscured by resolute silence. One early version suggested that Mrs. Jaques took the initiative by personally inviting him, even though he was not a member, to submit a group of etchings for the upcoming eighth annual Chicago Society of Etchers' exhibition in March of 1918.[1] Word of Winks' local reputation had probably reached her (she had been a nonresident member of the California Society since 1913) and she may have seen his work at the AIGA show in 1917, in which she was also an exhibitor. But Roi Partridge, Winks' longtime friend and fellow Western etcher, insisted otherwise. Established in his own career earlier than Winks and fairly bubbling in those days with etching camaraderie, in 1917 Partridge made a trek to San Francisco from Carmel specifically to meet John Winkler. Finding him in impoverished circumstances at the Glencliff and completely won over by the sparkle of Winks' personality, Partridge steered the conversation to etchers' talk. Winks obliged by showing his plates and, more impressed than he had expected to be, Partridge demanded to know what Winks was doing with them. "I'm not doing anything with them. Sometimes I put an acid bottle down on a plate and it makes a ring." Outraged, Partridge bellowed back, "Oh, don't *do* that. It ruins the plate! You must put these on the market. You *must* send them to Bertha Jaques."[2] According to Partridge, Winks did.

However it happened, Winks' connection with Jaques was the most important event in his career after his fortuitous enrollment at the Institute. By 1918, Jaques' influence in the American etching community was plenary, and she herself had become such an institution that the inner circles had universally reduced her name to the final abbreviation, "BJ." Given her concern for Winks' reputation even as late as the 1930s, it is apparent that Jaques was deeply affected by his work from her earliest contact with it. In fact, she may have been the ultimate source of the frequent comparisons to Whistler, for among all the etchers she knew— and it was her life to know them all—she regarded John W. Winkler as one of the very few truly possessed of greatness.

Though Winks and Bertha Jaques would not meet face to face until the fall of 1921, by early 1918 they had embarked on a correspondence that grew to weekly or even more frequent exchanges. With grace and decorum Winks shared his victories, discouragements, and the countless details of his work with her. Jaques in return sent encouragement, all manner of technical advice, and shared her considerable wisdom regarding the conduct and management of an etching career. She also provided Winks with the finest supplies, including rare or exotic oriental papers, for which he reciprocated by forwarding her the trial proofs of his new plates as well as formal issued prints for her private collection. And if she behaved on occasion with a touch of the patron, he was quick to respond with a touch of the poet. For the next five years Winks would enjoy nothing better than surprising her with the newest flight of his etcher's fancy. At base, it was the warmest of working relationships. And Jaques, with absolute confidence in her own assessment of Winkler's work, took up the matter of his reputation and the promotion and sale of his work almost as a personal cause.

———————————

In early 1918 Winks sent a few proofs to the Chicago Society of Etchers, doubtless forwarding his best prints from the 1917 plates. The jury accepted the very respectable number of six, weighting the representation toward the Chinatown images.[3] The real surprise came, however, when *Gingershop* captured one of the Chicago Society's four coveted Logan prizes, worth $25 in currency but invaluable in terms of prestige and publicity. Though Jaques certainly had a hand in this, the Society's jury was not a rubber stamp. The prize represented the genuine admiration of the etching community for Winks' work. In company with William A. Levy (Roi Partridge's mentor), Ernest D. Roth, and J. C. Vondrous (the Czech-born Logan prize winner for 1917), John Winkler had finally arrived. And he would win the Logan prize again in 1919 and once more in 1920, making of him somewhat of a phenomenon among America's junior etchers. Shortly after his triumph with *Gingershop*, and no doubt as a direct consequence, Winks plunged headlong into the arena of print club shows, taking up the burdensome tasks of nearly perpetual printing, matting, packing, and shipping which this national level of exposure and competition necessitated. He showed five Chinatown images at the Brooklyn Society of Etchers' 1918 exhibition, and in August, at the annual exhibition of the California Society in San Francisco, he presented *Delicatessen* [Maker], *Gingershop, Chowseller, Chinatown—San Francisco,* and *Under the Awning.* Thus, with the Logan prize to his credit and the strong showing in San Francisco, Winks began to attract the attention of promoters and dealers.

E. H. Furman of San Francisco's premier graphic arts gallery, The Print Rooms, apparently arrived first with an offer of representation at the standard fifty percent for new etchers,[4] and with a plan for promoting Winks' work that included a first one-man show in February of 1919. With increasing receipts from Bertha Jaques and the promise of income from The Print Rooms, Winks was at last in a position to resign his lamplighting post. Characteristically, as he moved away from the days of scarcity he seems not to have looked back. And he evidently experienced none of the misgivings felt by his fellow etchers about entrusting one's economic future to the etching craze.[5] Winks was an *artist,* and it was in the scheme of things that he should live from his art. In any event, in 1918 his spirits were understandably high. So high, in fact, that he did a most uncharacteristic thing.

———————————

Nora Crowe, thirty-one at the time of her marriage to Winks, was the older sister of Louise Crowe, who had entered the San Francisco Institute of Art in September of 1913, one year behind Winks. Old photographs of SFIA parties show Nora, a talented and devoted violinist who may have been musically trained in Europe, as a participant in Institute social events and she and Winks undoubtedly met there. (Daughters of a wealthy Seattle shipbuilding family, the Crowe sisters had received the best of fine arts educations. In 1914, the household had been moved to Carmel to enable Louise to attend William Merritt Chase's summer painting classes there.[6] In Seattle they had attended elementary school with Imogen Cunningham, who later married Roi Partridge; in fact, it was Nora who sent Partridge to San Francisco to meet John Winkler in 1917.)

Even though we know nothing of their courtship, and very little of their subsequent relationship, we do know that Winks married a woman of "appropriate" social status and an artist in her own right. And although the most Winks would ever say about Nora in later years was "she was a very fine wife," there is reason to think he was very happily married in the beginning.[7] Nora shared Winks' career by assisting with correspondence and bookkeeping and the social calendar, and Winks shared Nora's career by taking up the viola, which he played in quartets with her into the late 1930s, even after their separation. But on such scanty information as Winks divulged, it is impossible to gauge Nora's impact on his art. However, in one of the very few etched portraits Winks attempted, he pictured Nora sitting on the porch of their apartment at 728 Pine Street as she quietly reads a book. She definitely belongs in that space. Without her, the prospect from the porch would have been drab indeed.

———————————————————————

1. "A New Star Is Born," *Christian Science Monitor*, November 20, 1920.

2. Taped interview with Roi Partridge by Elizabeth Ginno Winkler, July 1979, Winkler Archives.

3. *Clay Hill, Gingershop, Chowseller, Delicatessen Maker, On the Mud Flats,* and *Mission Street Wharf, San Francisco. An Exhibition of Etchings* (Chicago: The Art Institute of Chicago, 1918).

4. Furman's commission was renegotiated to one-third in early 1921. Winkler to Bertha Jaques, March 7, 1921, Winkler Archives.

5. For example, Roi Partridge had written Carl Smalley as early as 1913 saying, ". . . there surely is a growing craze for etchings all over the world, but doubtless more particularly in America. It is up to you and me representing respectively the handler and the producer to feather our nests while the thing is at its height. I for my part will attempt to see to it that while I labor to feather my nest I may gain the while such a skill of hand that a good income is assured after the craze

is passed." Partridge to Smalley, May 19, 1913, Carl J. Smalley Papers, Breitweiser Art Archives, Santa Barbara, Calif.

By the time the etching market collapsed, Winkler's colleagues had arranged other careers: Roi Partridge had taken a position at Mills College, John Taylor Arms went into editorial work for art journals, and Arthur Heintzelman became Keeper of Prints for the Boston Public Library. Winkler, however, remained an etcher.

6.   Louise Crowe became a painter of some distinction, residing in Santa Fe for a good portion of her career. Edan Milton Hughes, *Artists in California 1786–1940* (San Francisco: Hughes Publishing, 1986), p. 108.

7.   "There is no doubt whatever we were happy in our marriage. What broke it up were a lot of threads that became a rope, to unravel it would be useless." Winkler to John Taylor Arms, November 6, 1948, Winkler Archives.

Nora Crowe 1917. Red conte crayon

North End of Telegraph Hill 1918

7. *For Winkler, however, San Francisco was more than a precious inspiration of so many charming etchings, it was also the kindly force which showed him the way of his destiny and made of him an artist.* Louis Godefroy, "The Etchings of J.W. Winkler" in *The Print Connoisseur,* July 1924

John Winkler loved success. So perfectly did his personality blend with the role of the modern painter-etcher that no one who later knew him could seriously doubt that the years between 1918 and 1928 constituted the very best of his nine decades. With self-doubt banished and personal dissonances subdued, Winks apparently so enjoyed the praise and attention that he groped for ways to keep on an even keel. His responses included both grand gestures and stern disciplines. On the one hand, he traded $600 of the $685 total proceeds from his first one-man show for Rembrandt's etching *The Triumph of Mordecai,*[1] which he hung over his work table at 728 Pine Street and thus, according to a later report, "when he found himself suffering from what he called 'over-confidence,' it was only necessary to raise his eyes to the work of the master etcher and he would in a spirit of reverence and humility recommence his labors."

On the other hand, militant against what he believed to be the deadly effects of complacency, Winks patrolled his consciousness for traces of conceit, growing ever more severe in his judgment of his own work.[2] In doing this he appears to have internalized what was actually an objective condition of his recently acquired status. Perhaps because he took for granted the painter-etcher's capacity for "spontaneous" creation, he did not clearly recognize that inherent in his role as America's brightest painter-etcher lurked a relentless pressure continually to produce works which were at once excellent and *new.* Whether or not he acknowledged the pressure Winks felt it deeply, and in the early phase of his national acclaim he met the challenge head on.

As a student (probably in early 1915) Winks had etched on Telegraph Hill, which he seems to have regarded at that time as a logical part of his *Views of San Francisco* series. No record survives to tell us why he returned there with his grounded plates and stylus in 1918, but, like the Oakland estuary, Telegraph Hill was recognized in West Coast art circles as extremely picturesque subject matter for any *plein air* artist, regardless of the medium.[3] At that time, the hill was a mixed community of Italian and Spanish peoples, although its European ethnicity was not nearly so compelling to Winks as Chinatown's exotic orientalism. It was not so much the population as the hill itself that fascinated him, the hill and the numerous manifestations of the human condition perched upon its rocky mass.

In each of the eighteen plates Winks created on Telegraph Hill (where no one cared enough to draw a blind against his inquiring eye), he spoke in varying degrees of the same basic elements: namely, that it was a *hill*, precipitous in spots and often providing spectacular overviews of the bay and San Francisco's wharves; that the dwellings on the hill reflected the individuals who inhabited them and expressed in their rambling, sometimes precarious forms countless acts of accommodation between the will of the fishing community to live there and the stubborn resistance of the rock; that whatever hardships or deprivations had been visited upon this community it was nevertheless thriving since there were inquisitive, happy children everywhere; and finally, that the hill bore its mantle of human colonization lightly, for it harbored a sizeable number of chickens and unbelieveable numbers of those intriguing mountain climbers, goats.

In their marvelous spaciousness and loving detail, Winks' Telegraph Hill plates achieved the "vibration of light and air" and the "kinetic effect" he said he had been striving for.[4] And many of them seem as near effortless as etchings could possibly be. *North End of Telegraph Hill*—perhaps the best and certainly the most famous of these plates—was executed in one day, directly and perfectly at the scene. He never altered one line of it in all the years that followed. (Although the Telegraph Hill plates evidently were created with a special view toward a local audience,[5] those who seem to have enjoyed them most were not San Franciscans nor even Americans. In 1924, after Winks' show at the Guiot Galleries in Paris, the Parisians were drawn to them, seeing in the tumbledown shanties on the hill a distant reflection of their own beloved Montmartre. But in the early 1970s, when the etching craze had been dead for so long that no one remembered it *except* Winks—at that time himself the subject of a revival—it was the Telegraph Hill etchings that especially touched the hearts of modern San Franciscans and reminded the larger art world of the warmth of Winkler's legacy and, more particularly than any of his other work, the sunny aspects of his humor.)

As for the San Francisco print market, E. H. Furman represented Winks very well. The Print Rooms touted his work at every opportunity and local sales were booming. But as for the wider market, and particularly east coast buyers, Furman's range was woefully short, although in 1919 he did consign a number of Winkler prints to the well-respected print dealer Carl Smalley. Then based in McPherson, Kansas, Smalley was attempting to build a print house on the works of such contemporary printmakers as Gustave Bauman, Howell C. Brown, Carl Armin Hansen, Bertha Jaques, Bertha Boynton Lum, Helen Hyde, and John Taylor Arms. Considered highly ethical as a dealer, Smalley traveled widely, functioning as a "drummer" for the genre. Winks regarded him as "the small but honest man" and in late 1920 opted to deal directly through him. But Smalley was no better able than Furman to reach the eastern markets. Still, Winks was certainly a national commodity by early 1920 and so the question of the proper eastern representative needed to be resolved.

Of course, Bertha Jaques, through the Chicago Society, had served de facto as Winks' eastern representative from 1918 by constantly including his work in the many rotary shows the Society sent out, and by administering the sales from those exhibits. There was also considerable trade from eastern and international collectors who preferred to deal directly with Jaques and the Chicago Society's impressive reserve stock of prints. But the Chicago Society was a print dealer incidentally to its main purpose of promoting painter-etching, and Winks' reputation had outgrown the arena of the print clubs. Thus it may have been that Bertha Jaques took matters into her own hands in early 1920 by introducing Winks to the established Boston print house, Doll & Richards. This very professional firm eagerly undertook his eastern representation and immediately saw to it that Winks entered the local Massachusetts competition of the Concord Art Association (at which *Chowseller* took the highest prize in the etching category), and then scheduled a major exhibition in Boston for November of 1920, at the height of the eastern gallery season. For this event, unbeknownst to Winks, no less an American etching luminary than Frank W. Benson volunteered to write the foreword for the catalogue.[6]

If etching began for Winks "as a hobby," in six short years it had so consumed his energies that by 1919 it was not only his calling but also his way of life. With his infinite capacity for charm and his talented and beautiful wife, Winks was by then a leading personality in San Francisco's bohemian art colony. He and Nora circulated in the social orbit of The Print Rooms, which served for a brief period around 1920 as the center of the city's most progressive artists' network, attracting prominent western artists such as Roi Partridge and his photographer-wife Imogen Cunningham,[7] and Maynard Dixon and Dorothea Lange, who met there.[8]

Yet Winks and Nora let it be known as early as 1919 that they did not intend to remain in San Francisco but planned instead to relocate indefinitely to Europe. The impetus for this plan probably originated with Nora and gained strength from sister Louise's decision to further her art study in Paris. It is unlikely that Winks would have decided on his own to go back to Europe, placing himself in uncomfortable proximity to Vienna. His noncommittal explanation, "I wanted to see what the war had done," suggests no overriding artistic motive. The European tour, which was virtually mandatory for American-born etchers, held no special appeal for him even though he owed as much if not more than the others to Paris, the birthplace of modern painter-etching. And while he actually discovered considerable etching inspiration when he finally arrived in France, Winks displayed no advance interest in the portrayal of western Europe for American consumption, the enterprise that preoccupied his American contemporaries. But it must also be said that Winks did not resist the move, and in the familiar spirit of adventure he probably looked forward to it. So the plans existed from an early date but the implementation lagged. One reason for the delay may have been Winks' citizenship status. He had entered the United States on forged papers, and it was not until May 16, 1921, that he was issued a certificate of naturalization, a prerequisite for his passport. However, most of the delay no doubt had to do with the intensification of Winks' career in the winter of 1920 and the spring of 1921.

That season took shape as a glittering succession of exhibitions. Besides the major November show in Boston, Winks would also exhibit with the Concord (Massachusetts) Art Association and the Brooklyn Society of Etchers, and in December, in Los Angeles, his first one-man show in southern California would open. The Chicago Society of Etchers' eleventh annual took place in late January (two months earlier than usual), followed closely by the Los Angeles Print Makers' second international on March 1. And the Minneapolis firm of J.S. Bradstreet had proposed a one-man exhibition for April. Since Winks insisted on personally executing every task associated with the production of his etchings, as well as packing and shipping, which if not done correctly might destroy the images by creasing the fine oriental papers on which they were printed, this schedule translated directly into a mountain of work. But Winks still found time to keep up his connection with the California Society, serving on various juries in 1920 and 1921, though not exhibiting with them because the rules barred him from further competitive exhibition after his receipt of the top prize in 1919.

Winks had about six months between the Chicago Society's March of 1920 exhibit and the opening of his November show in Boston. He used the time primarily to make new plates, and by October was able to ship to Doll & Richards fifty-one fine prints from the existing portfolio, augmented by a group of eleven plates which he designated "never before shown."[9] These plates included *Idle Hour, Oriental Cobbler, Small Delicatessen Booth,* and *Sing Fong.* (He also created but did not exhibit a new series of Chinatown alleys, notably *Oriental Alley* and *Light Alley.* The major Chinatown triumph, however, was *Awnings and Balconies,* a detailed street panorama instantly recognized as a major plate by The Print Rooms and others.) Concurrently with the Chinatown studies, Winks pursued his work in progress on Telegraph Hill, completing three plates in time for the Boston show: *Cottages on Telegraph Hill, Old Wharves of San Francisco,* and the superb *Fisherman's Home on Telegraph Hill,* to the evolution of which Bertha Jaques had contributed her opinions.[10] Finally, and as if to epitomize his old *Views of San Francisco* project, Winks created the breathtaking vista *View from Nob Hill.*

Evidently bedazzled by Winks' Boston show, the *Christian Science Monitor* of November 29, 1920 announced that "a new star" had appeared. Illustrated with a three-column reprint of *Gingershop,* the *Monitor* article foreshadowed the tone of American press commentary on Winks' work for

Oriental Alley 1920

a decade to come. Incredulous at the achievement of one so young and so new to the etching medium, the reviewer wondered aloud what the future held for an artist who had *premiered* with works that rivaled Whistler and Rembrandt. And the Boston *Evening Transcript* chimed in, heralding Winks as the "artist laureate of San Francisco, very much as Meryon was for Paris."[11] Although such sentiments would harden into cliché by the end of the decade, and Winks himself would find emptiness in their repetition, in 1920 they genuinely expressed the American public's warmest admiration for his work. Public excitement about the place he had already achieved and confidence in his promise were rendered palpable in the first of many institutional purchases following the Boston show. Winks wrote to Bertha Jaques that Mr. Risi of the Library of Congress had purchased "a number of my etchings for his department," and noted what he probably regarded as a higher compliment: "He also asked me for prints for his own collection."[12]

By the time of the Minneapolis show in April of 1921, Winks was planning an August departure for Paris and fretting that he would have to "use every minute of the day and parts of the night" to get through his work.[13] But out of a heavy printing schedule designed to create a substantial reserve of prints, and out of the little remaining time he had to store up his last impressions of Chinatown, he marshaled his energies for one final exhibition. The Print Rooms had scheduled a major retrospective and farewell celebration for July, to mark "The culmination of Mr. Winkler's San Francisco series." This exhibition and private sale of etchings was indeed the grand finale, for Winks showed over sixty images, just a handful fewer than his portfolio of issued prints. Though regretting the imminent loss of "one of the best known members of San Francisco's art colony," the *Chronicle* underscored the significance of the show: "Not since Joseph Pennell's etchings of the city were exhibited here in 1915 has such a large and important group of San Francisco subjects been shown."[14] And this showing prompted an act of appreciation from the State of California which must have particularly gratified Winks. On the wise counsel of state librarian Milton J. Ferguson,[15] fine print connoisseur and public patron of the graphic arts, the California State Library purchased fifty-seven prints for its collection, or every image in the exhibit except those it had already acquired through the Los Angeles Print Makers.[16] The San Francisco portfolio, representing eight years' labor and the development of a master American etcher, had found a suitable home.

*Fisherman's Home on
Telegraph Hill* c.1920–1922

Awnings and Balconies 1920

Winks and Nora boarded the train for the East Coast on schedule, with a stop planned for Chicago where Winks would finally meet Bertha Jaques, and with several weeks reserved for New York, where he would initiate arrangements with the prestigious print house of Frederick Keppel. The future could not have looked more promising. Never doubting that the momentum of his career would survive the relocation to France, Winks packed up perhaps fifty unbitten and unprinted plates of San Francisco subject matter, a cushion of new material by which he could (and did) perpetuate his exhibition obligations for several years to come.

Winks seems not to have thought that the move to Paris could result in a serious loss. The inspiration San Francisco had provided should travel easily, like his needles and his copper plates. But the loss to come would have to do with time and place—the chemistry of Winks' own interaction with the city of San Francisco when both were young. As the future would reveal, etching the city from memory could not substitute for the spontaneous recording of a living impulse. The San Francisco plates Winks issued sporadically from Paris between 1922 and 1924, though excellent etchings, did not convey that subtle quality of free and personal expression which so distinguished the Winkler images as they had evolved through the year 1920. When Winks left San Francisco in 1921, he abandoned forever his silent partner in the painter-etcher enterprise. The face of San Francisco would change, and when Winks returned he was a different man. And so, the most productive era of his creative life had come to an end.

1. "Report of Sales to J. W. Winkler," The Print Rooms, March 1, 1920; Arthur H. Millier, "California's Etchers," *Los Angeles Times* (?), April 1927 (?); Winkler Archives.

2. For this latter trait Bertha Jaques chided him in 1923: "You cannot convince me that anything you do is not successful—even if it happens not to please you. It is possible to become hypercritical and that is what has happened to you. Trust yourself more and let a plate stand when your first impulse lags and then you won't go on and spoil it as you say you have the *Gingershop*." Jaques to Winkler, October 8, 1923, Winkler Archives.

3. Roi Partridge had written an article in which he gave a description of the place, hoping to lure oil painters to the eucalyptus trees and ruined dance hall at

Old Wharves of San Francisco 1919

the crest of Telegraph Hill: "Indeed there is more than picturesqueness about Telegraph Hill to remind one of Italy: It has a strong resemblance to the rocky crests upon which feudal Italy was wont to build its villages. . . . On the way up today there are loud smells . . . and dirt (I mean litter), and lastly there are great numbers of Italian children . . . there are sewers that cross the street on top (oh, hold your nose in passing); there is washing hanging out everywhere save on the backs of men . . . down below are great quays. . . . Someday the San Francisco Park Board will plant a lawn up there and flowers primly in beds. And then it will be a park. Now it is just Telegraph Hill." "Little Italy on Telegraph Hill," *Seattle Town Crier*, July 28, 1917.

4. "At present [Winkler's] work is entering a new phase. I have just had the pleasure of spending several evenings at his studio and we talked it over thoroughly. As he expresses it, many of his former plates were 'static.' That is his attention was devoted to beauty in line and spot arrangement, a *pattern*, rather than life. Now, led by his great love for Rembrandt, he is striving for vibration of light and air, for a 'kinetic' effect, and how well he will succeed may be seen in his *Oriental Cobbler* and *Sing Fong*." Howell C. Brown, "John W. Winkler—An Appreciation," *The American Magazine of Art* 12 (June 1921): 187–191.

5. Winkler may well have made the first Telegraph Hill plates especially for his one-man exhibition at The Print Rooms in February of 1919, for they were advertised as his "new etchings" in connection with that exhibition. Anna C. Winchell, *San Francisco Chronicle*, February 9, 1919.

    At the California Society of Etchers eighth annual exhibition in August of 1919, he showed four Telegraph Hill etchings "from a new series depicting scenes from Telegraph Hill." "Artists and Their Work," *San Francisco Chronicle*, August 3, 1919.

6. When Winkler saw the catalogue, he wrote immediately to Benson to thank him. Benson replied: "I should not have been able to write that foreword for your catalogue unless I had genuinely enjoyed your etchings. I was very much struck with them the first time I saw them and always look forward with pleasure to any opportunity of seeing them." Benson to Winkler, December 15, 1920, Winkler Archives.

7. Interestingly, the bond Winkler established in these days with Imogen Cunningham deepened significantly after he returned from Europe in the late 1920s. Both as friend and fellow artist, Imogen had enjoyed him in the early days when his disposition was bright, but it was the darker moods he expressed after his return that attracted her camera. In the early 1930s she produced a splendid portrait series which Winkler greatly appreciated. Imogen once said to him: "If you were laughing in front of my camera, I wouldn't take it. And I will tell you,

I don't think laughing expresses you in any case. We always talked about very serious matters. The more bitter I could get you, the better I liked it." Taped conversation between John and Elizabeth Winkler, and Imogen Cunningham, n.d., Winkler Archives.

8.   Wesley M. Burnside, *Maynard Dixon, Artist of the West* (Provo, Utah: Brigham Young University Press, 1974), pp. 66–67.

9.   *Invitation to an Exhibition and Private Sale of Etchings by John W. Winkler* (Boston: Doll & Richards, 1920): Doll & Richards Exhibition Catalogs 1912–1941, roll NDR1, frames 362–363, Archives of American Art, Smithsonian Institution.

10.   Sometime in late 1920 Winkler had evidently written to Jaques that he was working on *Fisherman's Home*. She may at that time have seen only the small trial proof that he had sent. In any event, she wrote back urging him not to interfere with what she called "the tangle" in the image, an apparent reference to the complexity in her own image *The Tangle, Chioggia*. Winkler responded: "The tangle in *Fisherman's House* [Winkler's earliest name for this etching] will not be lessened nor removed. Never. However I am making the plate over again and am trying to get a more compact composition. There will be another tangle in close approximation of the old one." Winkler to Jaques, April 13, 1921, Winkler Archives.

11.   W. H. Downes, Boston *Evening Transcript*, November 11, 1920.

12.   Winkler to Jaques, January 19, 1921, Winkler Archives.

13.   Winkler to Jaques, May 8, 1921, Winkler Archives.

14.   Norma Abrams, "Artists and Their Work," *San Francisco Chronicle*, July 10, 1921.

15.   Milton J. Ferguson was California state librarian from 1917 to 1930. He was an honorary member of the Print Makers Society of California and the California Society of Etchers. Howell C. Brown praised Ferguson's contribution to the graphic arts in California, attributing to him the formulation of a buying plan for the state library that limited expenditure on the acquisition of old masters and applied the bulk of the available funds to the purchase of works by living artists. After building a splendid collection of California graphic art, Ferguson went to the Brooklyn Library in 1930.

16.   *Book Orders* vols. 41335–46256 and 46257–51224, California State Archives, California State Library, Sacramento, Calif.

View from Nob Hill 1920

Les abandonnés, Paris, 1925

8. *To John W. Winkler: One of the finest etchers I know, whom I class with Rembrandt and of whom he makes me think.*
Bertha Jaques, flyleaf inscription, 1934

It was perhaps because John Winkler lacked an artistic agenda when he moved to Paris that his six-year residence there produced uneven work and increasingly debilitating emotional turmoil. He had changed locations almost casually, with no real understanding that anything else in his life might be affected. Geographically and culturally distant from the environment that had nurtured him, Paris would not allow him to continue the creative life he had known.

Winks' stay in France began with an illness that dampened his spirits and played havoc with his shortrange plans. Just after he and Nora had taken living quarters in the Paris suburb of Clamart, Winks fired off a directive to his American representatives enacting across-the-board increases in the market price of his prints.[1] His intention was probably to bolster his income in order to purchase time for a creative vacation from the San Francisco portfolio. But the letters had scarcely been delivered when Winks found himself in the American Hospital of Paris for what turned out to be a forty-one day bout with typhoid fever—the result, he later thought, of eating pastries from the fly-covered outdoor offerings of the Parisian bakeries. This serious illness, from which he did not fully recover until July of 1922, seemed to set the tone for his personal reaction to France, which he found "backward" and repugnantly filthy.

Following recovery, for the remainder of 1922 Winks worked almost exclusively on the San Francisco plates. He finished several from the store of impressions he brought along and "remade" a number of the images that were already on the market.[2] The previous plates no longer satisfied him; at the very least, he thought, the technical presentation could be greatly improved. Further, and undoubtedly with Nora's assistance, Winks maintained his American exhibition schedule for 1922, participating in the annual shows of the Chicago, Los Angeles, Concord, and Brooklyn print clubs. He garnered no prizes but the entire San Francisco set was so well established by then that its images could not, realistically, be considered competitive.

Perhaps deliberately fostering the impression that all was as he had expected, in the late fall he reported to Bertha Jaques that "I am working continuously and things are progressing very rapidly."[3] But much of this was personal theater, a kind of optimistic charade conducted with Winks' customary bravado, to obscure the unsettling development of serious doubts and unetcherly artistic impulses. For in the same letter to Jaques he conveyed an astonishing decision, one that would deeply affect his etching career and involve him in a chain of consequences which would literally reverberate through each of his remaining fifty years. He announced to her his firm intention to "stop exhibiting for some time to come," and said he had so informed his commercial representatives in the United States.[4] But Winks' subsequent behavior was inconsistent with this stance. He did withdraw from the annual round of print club shows, the only national showcase for the current work of American etchers. And after 1922 he allowed his various memberships to lapse and restricted his club exhibitions to the Chicago and Brooklyn societies, continuing with these two solely out of personal devotion to their respective secretaries, Bertha Jaques and John Taylor Arms. However, he did not in fact forbid Doll & Richards and Frederick Keppel from exhibiting his issued works. Doll & Richards put on a second Winkler show in 1922, and Frederick Keppel juggled gallery schedules with etcher Arthur Heintzelman in order to present a major Winkler exhibition in December of 1923.

Winks' decision to cease exhibiting could be divined only if one understood that he equated exhibiting with the production of new work. His quandary resided in the conflict between his heartfelt desire to fulfill what the etching world had heralded as his "promise" and his growing resistance to the manufacture of more plates along the lines of the San Francisco portfolio, with which he was now disenchanted and, frankly, a little bored. Winks wanted to create plates that were not just better but unique and entirely different from any of his previous work. Perhaps encouraged by an innate streak of arrogance to believe that artistic transcendence was more or less an act of will, Winks proved ill equipped to withstand the battering waves of despair driven home by repeated failure to achieve such a goal. Yet he single-mindedly adhered to the idea and, like the drinker of hemlock, slowly succumbed to a creative paralysis which he could never, thereafter, entirely shake off. Though he made approximately fifty plates in France, and though some were brilliant, neither the French plates nor the subsequent London plates amounted to a "set"; they followed, but they did not rival, the San Francisco portfolio.

From every perspective, Winks' decision to stop exhibiting was a stunning professional error, yet the American etching community did not intervene. Even his perennial confidante, Bertha Jaques, was slow to express her opinion, perhaps unwilling to tread too heavily on the artistic process of another. But in October of 1923 she responded with empathy to his apparent despair: "The thought of you being depressed and not satisfied with your work makes me wish for an aeroplane that I might fly over there and talk to you. You cannot convince me that anything you do is not successful—even if it happens not to please you. I believe you are right about working too steadily at etching. You are progressing in technique by such steady work, but overdrawing your inspiration . . . . When you wrote to me of your new prices, I felt moderately sure they were too high for here and certain they were too high for Paris; but of course you had to find that out for yourself. I grant that very high prices are paid for etchings, but not until the etcher becomes so well established that collectors will have his work at any price—and you had not reached that point, but were rapidly reaching it, when you withdrew your prints from all but Keppel and Furman."[5]

If Winks discerned the note of disappointment and gentle censure in her letter, he did not acknowledge it. Eyes forward, he wrote back: "I am busy trying to regain certain things which I nearly forgot in the course of my long specialization in etching; I felt the ground was slowly slipping from under me and that I was in danger of becoming what I dread most of all, that is, a narrow specialist."[6]

Winks may have wished to transform his etching style or possibly to get out of etching altogether, but if so Paris impeded such longings at every turn, straightaway providing him with two new friends whose combined influence enmeshed him further in the American etching world. Already established in his Paris studio when Winks arrived, Arthur W. Heintzelman took an instant liking to his compatriot, whom Carl Smalley's letters had urged him to greet. A steadfast friendship developed

La marchande endormie 1923

out of the enthusiasm of the times and the magic of Paris,[7] and Arthur and Katherine's home would serve Winks more than once as a safe harbor in his turbulent years in France. Also a client-etcher of Frederick Keppel & Co., Heintzelman held a deep admiration for Winks' work.[8] And Winks, although discreetly reserving judgment on the overt sentimentality of Heintzelman's subject matter, readily acknowledged his skill. Winks and Nora often enlivened the Heintzelman dinner table and salon, and the two families were inseparable on holiday occasions. When this small society was augmented by the periodic visits of John Taylor Arms and his wife, Dorothy Noyes, a different and even higher spirit prevailed. Arms brought the ardor of his personality and his unabashed passion for etching to the group. He had admired Winks from his position as secretary of the Brooklyn Society of Etchers before they first met at New York's Commodore Hotel in the fall of 1921, and for Winks, Arms was the shining example of everything an etcher should be.

Between 1922 and 1925, when Arms was in Paris, this trio of American junior etchers often sallied forth together into the Latin Quarter, each searching out his own communion with the picturesque, and more often than not *plein air* etching within a stone's throw of each other.[9] Watching Winks work in the streets of Paris, Arms was smitten by his genius for the art of etching, epitomized, he felt, by the miraculous spontaneity of the creative act, resulting in the brilliant vitality of Winks' etched line.[10] Until his death in 1953, Arms treasured the memory of Winks creating the French scene *La marchande endormie,* of watching his needle fly over the plate in a race against time lest the sleeping woman should awaken and change her position. Arms drank in the purest inspiration from this experience, and a deep and abiding affection grew up between these two men, based in large part on Arms' loyalty to the mastery Winks had demonstrated. No matter how estranged from the world of etching John Winkler would subsequently become, John Taylor Arms would never allow him or the American print public to forget that genius.[11]

From Arms, Winks took inspiration of a different sort, alloyed, one senses, with the melancholy recognition that private disaffection prevented him from participating fully in Arms' artistic idealism. Arms had pursued his love of Gothic themes since 1915, had etched many of his famous gargoyles by 1919, and was just beginning his distinguished *French Cathedral Series* in 1923. So intimate was the creative bond between the two that Winks himself entered the Gothic spirit, perhaps for

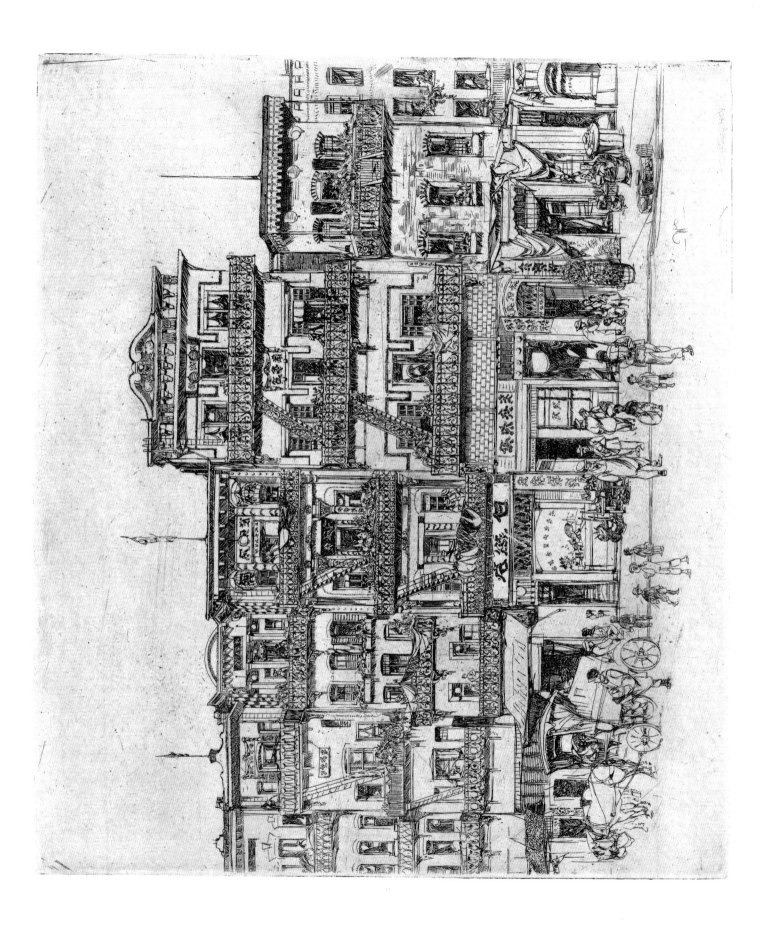

the sheer joy of the visual dialogue with his friend. The most remarkable products of this excursion are Winks' pencil drawings of various French cathedrals, representing a chapter in his artistic life which, like his pen and ink drawings of assorted figures, he did not acknowledge until the late 1940s.[12] Produced sporadically between 1923 and 1927, the cathedral drawings electrified Arms, who personally coveted them and feared that Winks did not value them sufficiently to ensure their survival. For years Arms begged to buy them and for an equal number of years Winks refused to sell them, finally gratuitously forwarding a package of drawings to Arms in 1948, from which Winks had reserved a number for inclusion in the corpus of his own work.[13]

Winks' encounter with Arms in the Gothic spirit also affected the San Francisco portfolio, already heavily imbued with Winks' own feeling for architectural rendition. No document survives to verify the connection, yet in light of the bond between the two etchers it is difficult to contemplate Arms' 1927 tour de force of Rouen Cathedral, *Lace in Stone*, without a mental cross-reference to Winks' marvelous Chinatown image, *Facades*. (Probably sketched out in 1921, the unfinished plate was carried to Paris but its subsequent history is obscure. Like the cathedral drawings, the final etched version of *Facades* appeared first in the early 1950s when, as Winks was fond of pointing out, he had finally "come to his senses.") In any event, the relationship between John Taylor Arms and John Winkler was artistically productive on both sides. Anchored in the high excitement of their days in France and fed thereafter by the constancy of Arms' affection, this friendship was for Winks the finest gift which Paris gave him.[14]

Though Winks' subterranean doubts and creative rebellions joined forces very soon after he arrived in France, on the surface he continued in the painter-etcher mode, achieving almost in spite of himself the same type of charmed success in western Europe that he had recently experienced in America. By the end of 1923 Winks had created a group of etchings which concentrated on the street merchants of the Latin Quarter.[15] Similar in spirit to his 1917 Chinatown studies, these etchings featured individual figures with no attempt to depict the urban landscape of Paris. The seller of birds, the garlic merchant, the book dealer, each engrossed in commerce, stand apart from their surroundings, dignified to a degree by the purity of the space around them. And Winks had allowed the subjects

Facades c.1920–1921

Le grand brocanteur, Paris c.1926

to remain apart, biting and printing the *plein air* plates without corrective alteration or background elaboration.

Initially these plates may have been mere experiments in search of a different style. The merchant etchings were sketches, hurriedly recorded on the impulse of the moment, and Winks certainly had no grand plans for them. Yet even without so much as a line to indicate location the figures are eloquent with the spirit of Paris. They could belong to no other place. Probably at Arms' urging, they were published and sold in America through the Chicago and Brooklyn societies and at Frederick Keppel. They also gained ready recognition in France, where their existence meant that the Parisian etching community could lay a modest claim not only to Winks' fellowship but also to his genius.

Because the little wooden press Winks had at home in Clamart could not produce the volume of prints necessary to meet the market demand for the San Francisco portfolio, one of Winks' early missions in Paris had been to locate a suitable printer. Making straight for the source, he searched out the fine printing establishment of the younger Eugène Delâtre, whose father was enshrined in the annals of the painter-etcher as Whistler's printer. When the employees proved unable to print the San Francisco images to the exacting standards of their client, the spectacle of Winks' own virtuoso printing performances edified the shop. And it may have been through Delâtre's establishment that Winks had become acquainted with the leading Parisian printmaking association, *La société internationale de la gravure originale en noir*, and its most influential *sociétaire*, Louis Godefroy. Etcher, critic, and fine art dealer, Godefroy took up Winks' cause with affection and energy, like others before him. Widely regarded as the elite of French printers, the *société* staged periodic exhibitions at Galeries Simonson, where Winks, as a member elect, was invited to exhibit in January of 1924.[16] By that time, however, Godefroy was putting the finishing touches on bigger plans. He was looking forward to a major exhibition of Winks' work at the gallery of his business partner, Marcel Guiot, and beyond that he anticipated the publication of what he hoped would be the definitive article on the images, accompanied by what Winkler collectors on both sides of the Atlantic had been clamoring for, a rudimentary *catalogue raisonné*.[17]

Except for the one-man exhibitions at The Print Rooms in 1919 and 1921, Winks had never been in a position to attend his major openings. But in March of 1924, at Guiot's gallery on rue Volney, he was present to relish the event and to hear with modest astonishment the accolades of

Albert Besnard, distinguished artist and director of the Ecole des Beaux-Arts, whose visit to the gallery marked the high point of the exhibition. An even higher honor was paid when the French government purchased four Winkler prints for the permanent collection of the Musée du Luxembourg.[18] And in spite of Winks' growing distaste for press "stories," news of this exhibition was featured in American newspapers, resulting in a flurry of sales at Keppel's in New York. Three months later the prestigious international graphic art journal *The Print Connoisseur* carried Godefroy's enthusiastic article on Winkler's work,[19] illustrated with an impression of *La marchande de légumes* as printed directly from the etching plate which Winks had contributed to the magazine. Then, toward the end of the year, Malcolm C. Salaman, who, as editor of the annual compilation *Fine Prints of the Year*, virtually dictated the taste of the British print public,[20] made overtures to Winks on behalf of the leading London print house, H.C. Dickins. Winks concluded arrangements with that firm for international representation in early 1925. Generously, Salaman also offered to introduce Winks to England with a monograph projected to follow the London gallery debut.[21]

Buoyed by the warmth of his reception in Paris and Guiot's healthy sales, and temporarily relieved of financial worries by a $10,000 advance from Dickins, it appeared as if Winks had risen above the Paris malaise. In May of 1925, he and Nora traveled to London for business meetings with Dickins, who personally took the opportunity to introduce Winks to the Thames with entertainments that included a leisurely cruise up to Hampton Court. "First impressions of London and the river were wonderful," Winks noted in his journal, and in the euphoria of his enjoyment of the Thames (which had captivated Whistler himself some fifty years before) he projected another comprehensive series—a London set—and turned his full attention to the river and the life on its banks. In fact, less than a month after his arrival in London, he was spending entire days working on a plate of Waterloo Bridge.[22] Word of the newly awakened interest spread like wildfire among Winks' friends, who seemed relieved to hear that he had found himself again. And Arms wrote from Connecticut in June: "I can imagine you would be in perfect paradise anywhere along the Thames for there is certainly an infinite amount of material there of the kind you love to draw." Always the optimist, Arms looked forward to immediate results: "I would appreciate it a lot if you would send me a comprehensive group for the Brooklyn show opening November 1st. I will keep for myself all that I can afford to purchase and

the rest will go to the Exhibition."[23] But no London plates were issued in the fall of 1925, and Arms was still anticipating this work in 1928, when the first London plate, *Simon's Wharf*, appeared at the Chicago Society's February exhibition, and two more years would elapse before *From Bermondsey* and *Waterloo Bridge* were published.

Apparently, in the middle of 1925, on the banks of the Thames, where Winks had seemed so in tune with the old painter-etcher spirit, he entered a dark and private period nearly devoid of etching. He had evidently suffered a recurrence of the chilling doubt which had taken its toll in Paris. On the pencil sketch of two sail barges he addressed a "memo" to Arms: "I am now back where I was years ago, except that I have now what I did not have then—an awful knowledge that to the art of etching I contribute absolutely nothing."[24] And beyond the artistic crisis other difficulties came to the fore. Sensitive to French hostility toward Americans, Nora grew uncomfortable in Paris and in 1926 she went home, leaving Winks to attend to his European reputation by himself.[25] At first, he lingered with the Heintzelmans in Normandy, then traveled on and off to London to etch, with uncertain results. For a brief time, in 1927, he and Arms shared an artistic excursion to Rouen; this encounter may have prompted the completion of *Simon's Wharf*. By the end of 1927, however, it was clear that Winks desperately wanted out of etching. Nevertheless, it was his particular curse that no such option existed. His entire artistic history, bolstered by the severities of his mental makeup, required that he continue. Heavy with recriminations arising from nearly two consecutive "unproductive" years, Winks left Europe for California in January of 1928. He traveled alone, except for the cold companionship of the splendid etching press he had purchased in Paris—a symbol, perhaps, of his grim determination not to abandon the etcher's ship.

———————————

1. John W. Winkler, "New Price List," November 1922, Winkler Archives.

2. The remakes included: *Fruitstall, Noon Rest, Shrimp Wagon, Ross Alley,* and *View from Nob Hill.* He asked Bertha Jaques to "burn up" the old images of these plates in her possession. By late 1923 he had formulated a policy with respect to his public and the "new" plates. He wrote on the front inside cover of his pocket journal: "Any plate of the S.F. set that I made over should be exchanged for the old one if anybody wishes to have the new plate instead of the original one

regardless of a difference of the respective prices." Winkler to Jaques, November 29, 1922, and journal 1923 of John Winkler, Winkler Archives.

3. Winkler to Jaques, November 29, 1922, Winkler Archives.

4. "Did you receive my last letter in which I told you that I have stopped exhibiting for some time to come and asked you not to send any of my prints to exhibitions? I have also written to D. & R. about it and will also write to Keppel shortly."

5. Jaques to Winkler, October 8, 1923, Winkler Archives.

6. Winkler to Jaques, March 29, 1924, Winkler Archives. The American print-buying public as reflected in the activity of Winkler's various dealers was not so tolerant and American sales began to slip. Smalley was on the verge of bankruptcy by the end of 1922, and Furman, preoccupied with the impending move of The Print Rooms to Los Angeles, may have viewed Winkler's decision as a final straw, for it became clear by 1923 that Furman had turned against him and was not prepared to do anything further on his behalf. Abruptly, Winkler was without representation on the West Coast. Doll & Richards continued to sell what prints they had on hand, but received nothing to augment their supply after 1923. (A sales report of February 18, 1924, shows that Winkler had supplied them with a few of the French plates he produced in 1923. His net proceeds were $202.92, a figure which had fallen to $34.10 by the time of the next, and final, sales report in April of 1925.) And Frederick Keppel, to whom Winkler had turned for consolidation and direction of his American reputation during his sojourn abroad, was hamstrung by Winkler's decision, against which the top people in the firm had vigorously but vainly argued. With some disappointment Keppel reported that the one-man show in New York in the late winter of 1923 had garnered only a lukewarm response from the eastern critics: "Among the artists Mr. Pennell and Mr. Hassam were most enthusiastic as was also Bolton Brown. The press unfortunately did not give us the writeups that we had hoped for." C. F. Nicholas to Winkler, March 19, 1924, Winkler Archives.

7. Heintzelman referred to this period as "our glorious days in Paris; those formative years when rare and lasting friendships were made. . . . How well I remember your little wooden press with split roller. It was always a revelation to me how you could get fine prints from it regardless of what you say now, that they were not up to your present standard. Those are years that cannot be taken from us, and I realized this when Katherine and I were in Paris a few weeks ago. We walked up the rue Corneille beside the Odeon Theatre, passed our old hotel and had dinner at the restaurant 'Cochin aux Lait.' We made many pilgrimages

From Bermondsey, London 1925

into the Latin Quarter with thoughts of yesteryears. Paris has changed very little and when the train pulled out of the Gare St. Lazare there was a trace of a tear in both our eyes." Heintzelman to Winkler, April 9, 1952, Winkler Archives.

8.   Heintzelman subsequently became Keeper of Prints for the Boston Public Library, where he assembled a number of Winkler's prints within the Albert H. Wiggin Collection.

9.   Frederick Keppel put on a small exhibition of the French etchings of these three men in 1928.

10.   "I have watched Winkler standing (he never sits when working outdoors) in a crowded Paris street, wholly lost in his subject and oblivious of everyone and everything around him, the while his needle seemed to fly over the glossy black surface of the grounded plate tacked down on a small portfolio held in the crook of his left arm. I have seen him stand so by the hour, turning the portfolio first in one direction and then in another, while that nervous, staccato needle laid bare the glistening metal in a network of beautiful lines; and I have seen the composition grow—now in one part of the plate, now in another—until the whole lacelike mass finally came together in one homogeneous and well-related whole. At such times he never uses a preliminary sketch or drawing of any kind, and so keen is his sense of perspective, proportion and scale that the most intricate subject takes its place rightly and justly within the four bounding lines of the plate's edges. It all looks quite simple, yet it is, in reality, an extraordinary accomplishment." John Taylor Arms, "John W. Winkler, Master of Line," *Prints* 4 (January 1934): 4.

11.   The numerous activities John Taylor Arms undertook in furtherance of Winkler's reputation are too extensive to chronicle in detail. In the 1920s Arms, as secretary of the Brooklyn Society of Etchers, made sure Winkler was represented in the annual exhibitions and frequently entered his work in other exhibitions, irrespective of whether Winkler had "new" work to show and braving his displeasure. The Brooklyn Society thus became the vehicle for the introduction of the French etchings. Their eighth annual presented *La marchande endormie* and *Le petit brocanteur* in 1923, and the ninth annual featured *La bouquiniste*, *La marchande d'ail*, *Le petit Turc*, and *L'oiseleuse*, as well as the final version of *The Delicatessen Maker* which Winkler etched and printed in France. To maintain Winkler's reputation, Arms often drew from his own collection of Winkler prints. Arms' appreciative writing about him in the 1930s is well known.

12. An early exhibition of Winkler's French pencil drawings as well as the fine pen and ink sketches from Paris was presented by the California State Library in March of 1957. A perceptive reviewer commented: "The contrast in the style of drawing between the pencil work and the pen and ink is surprising. The pencil drawings are carefully executed . . . The pen and inks . . . are another matter. . . . The pen has sped across the surface of the paper as a skater skims across ice. As you can see, the usual roles of the pencil (the swift recorder of first impressions) and the pen (cantankerous recorder of the final decision) have been reversed. The pencil has become the serious scholar, the pen, a dashing cavalier. Winkler is a master draftsman—the kind who can make drawing seem like the only thing worth doing." John C. Oglesby, "Pencil, Ink Drawings By Winkler Show Master Hand," *Sacramento Bee*, March 14, 1957.

13. "I could have cried when you told me that that magnificent drawing you made of the Rouen doorway got ruined . . . you will remember how anxious I was to buy it in order that it might be preserved, for to me it was one of the most beautiful drawings I have ever seen." Arms to Winkler, June 29, 1927, Winkler Archives.

"I was intensely interested, John, in what you told me about the drawings you made of Gothic edifices. I would give my eye teeth to see them, for you were made to draw Gothic. How well I remember that wonderful drawing you made of the north door of St. Maclou—was it not? How I wanted that drawing, how I hinted and even begged! . . . Will you ever sell me one of your drawings?" Arms to Winkler, February 24, 1930, Winkler Archives.

14. "I remember distinctly our first meeting in the Commodore Hotel, also one very pertinent remark you made to me then. 'Once a friend, always a friend.' All these years I have not forgotten it and you have fully and in an overflowing measure lived up to it. Somehow John, '*mein geist*' has always been more akin to yours than to my other friends." Winkler to Arms, February 27, 1948, Winkler Archives.

15. The group includes: *Le petit marché, Les deux mendiants, Le vagabond, La bouquiniste, Le petit brocanteur, Le marchand Turc ambulant, Le petit Turc, La marchande de légumes, Le repos de l'ouvrier, Le marché à Montmartre, L'oiseleuse, Le marchand d'habits, La marchande endormie,* and *La marchande d'ail.*

16. "I have presented you to *La gravure originale en noir*! I gave your proofs to my friend Charles Jonas and gave him my ballot where you appeared at the head of the list. . . . As there were only five vacancies for fifteen candidates, the competition was particularly keen this year. But I received a letter this morning

from Jonas announcing that all my candidates were elected—sixteen votes for you and twelve for others. So, success, success! I am delighted. I hope you are not cross that I did this without asking your advice, but it pleased me to surprise you! The exhibit will take place at the end of January at Simonson." Godefroy to Winkler, November 17, 1923 (translation Annette Herskowitz), Winkler Archives.

17.   The "List of the Etchings of J.W. Winkler," which appears without comment at the conclusion of Louis Godefroy's article "The Etchings of J.W. Winkler," in the July 1924 issue of *The Print Connoisseur* (pp. 186–191), organizes 104 titles—1915 through and including 1923. To the present day this is the only comprehensive listing, and through the years collectors, scholars, and admirers have had no option except to rely upon its contents. In print, Godefroy notes that the list was furnished by Winkler. Godefroy knew better, however, since he had personally assigned to Nora Winkler the "little task" of establishing a list of all of Winkler's etched plates ordered by date of execution, including the dimensions of each plate and the state and the number in the edition. Godefroy to Winkler, January 7, 1924 (translation Annette Herskowitz), Winkler Archives.

Consequently, the list represents what Nora could pry out of Winkler which, not surprisingly, contains some omissions and some fantasies. For example, important omitted images include *Fisherman's Home on Telegraph Hill* and *Chinaman and Turtle.* Conversely, *The Dragon Balcony*, an allegedly large plate with an edition of 75, probably names a plate Winkler intended to make, since no image by that name has been found and no reference to this work appears anywhere in the voluminous Winkler Archives. Further, the asserted dates of creation of the images often do not correspond to other evidence which we now possess. And finally, the asserted editions are most likely an attempt to persuade collectors that Winkler adhered to the practice of numbered editions, a practice considered to increase the value of the individual print, whereas there is no credible evidence that Winkler printed numbered editions during or before 1923.

18.   The four prints were: *The Delicatessen Maker, Mission Street Wharf, Fisherman's Home on Telegraph Hill* and *Awnings and Balconies.* Winkler wrote: "Yesterday I received a letter from the Ministère des Beaux-Arts informing me that all of the four plates will go to the Luxembourg Museum; of course I am very pleased about it. I was under the impression that only one would be allotted to the Luxembourg and the rest distributed among the museums in the provinces." Winkler to Jaques, March 29, 1924, Winkler Archives.

19.   Louis Godefroy, "The Etchings of J.W. Winkler," *The Print Connoisseur* 4 (July 1924): 169–191.

20. Winkler later scribbled a comment on a letter he had received from Salaman in April of 1925: "Indeed, he swung a big axe; to get any metallic recognition in England it was necessary to have his axe turned away from me." Winkler Archives.

21. Malcolm Salaman, *The Etchings of John W. Winkler, 'Frisco to Montmartre* (London and New York: H.C. Dickins, 1925).

22. Journal of John Winkler, May 20 and June 10, 1925, Winkler Archives.

23. Arms to Winkler, June 25, 1925, Winkler Archives.

24. Pencil drawing of two sail barges near a bulwark on the Thames with a note "Memo to J.T.," n.d., Winkler Archives.

25. Upon her arrival in northern California, Nora took immediate steps to revive Winkler's West Coast market. She made arrangements with Vickery, Atkins & Torrey which commenced the sale of his works in October of 1926. The reports of sales of this firm show a good business in Winkler's San Francisco and French images through 1931. Nora also arranged a Winkler show at the San Francisco Institute of Art in 1927.

L'oiseleuse 1923

La bouquiniste 1923

Le petit marché, Paris c.1923

Forerunner to Winkler's French set of singular street merchants, *Vegetable Vendor* was needled in San Francisco in 1919 but, so far as is known, not issued then. He took the plate with him to Paris and printed it there as *Marchand de légumes au panier.*

Winkler produced some thirty "finished" pencil drawings (as opposed to the dozens of pencil sketches that were studies for etchings), many of them done August through October of 1927—in Paris, Rouen (where he was joined by John Taylor Arms), Joigny, and Caudebec-en-Caux. The drawings are freehand and, as with his *plein-air* etching, done while standing so that his right arm would have freedom of movement. He made virtually no erasures, first locating the primary (or controlling) intersections with dots and, when necessary, adding basic structural lines before tackling detail. Shaded areas were achieved with closely-spaced line, again as with the etchings. He concentrated almost entirely on architecture in the finished pencil work, and within that realm saved his most intense scrutiny for the great cathedrals. Nevertheless, trademark chickens, cats, and children were included wherever he could find the proper space.

The cathedral drawings—which are the centerpieces of the pencil work—usually took Winkler about three days to complete. In contrast, the furious spontaneity of the pen and inks suggest a two- or three-*minute* effort although we do not have Winkler's word on the matter. He used a steel pen, balancing the drawing board against his left side and holding the ink bottle with his left hand. As might be expected, he was partial to people and children on the streets and bistro-sitting characters, especially in Paris, but there are also quite a number of farm scenes and cityscapes—done at Rouen, Yvetot, Caudebec-en-Caux, in the Normandy countryside, and at Saint Valéry-en-Caux on the Normandy coast.

When he left Paris in January of 1928, Winkler was brooding over "nearly two consecutive unproductive years." In other words, he felt he had not created enough new etchings. Apparently, he did not value the drawings which, in the late 1930s or early 1940s, were saved from the round file by Roi Partridge.

The Senator in a bistro
Paris 1927. Pen and ink

Rouen — 1927

Rouen Cathedral Door
1927. Pencil—p. 122

Tour de Beurre—Rouen Cathedral
1927. Pencil—p. 123

Rouen with its Cathedrals
1927. Pencil

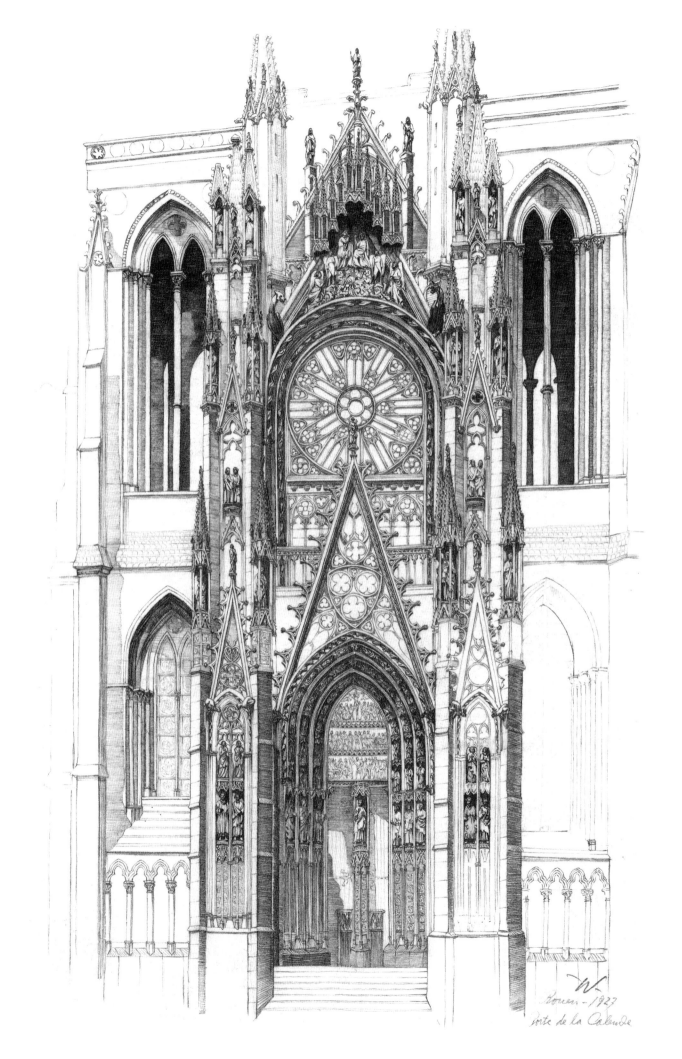

Rouen - 1927
Porte de la Calende

Cambridge Sept 4 - 97
"Porte du Tambour"

The White Chapel in the Hunting Lodge of Henry IV,
Caudebec-en-Caux. "I slept in this chapel August 4, 1927."

Porte de la Calende—Rouen Cathedral
1927. Pencil—p. 124

*Porte du Tambour—*Cathedral at
Caudebec-en-Caux 1927. Pencil—p. 125

Market Day, Caudebec-en-Caux 1927. Pencil

Women of Caudebec-en-Caux 1927. Pencil

Bistro group, Paris 1927. Pen and ink

Customer and Waitress, Paris 1927. Pen and ink

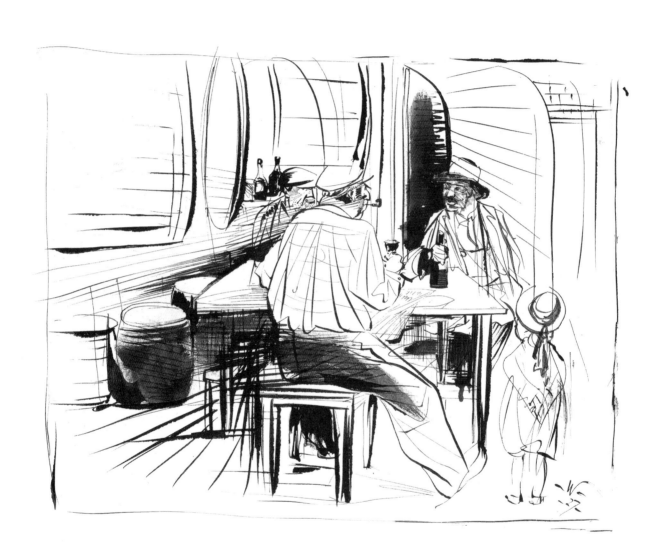

Characters in a bistro, Paris 1927. Pen and ink

In a wine cellar, Paris 1927. Pen and ink

Most of Winkler's Paris sketches were done in pencil, scattered willy-nilly across numerous and difficult-to-handle sheets of tissue paper. The rare pen-and-ink study here was done for the etching *Peddler Woman Weighing,* which never managed to compare to the drawing.

Two Windows in the
Dragon Court, Paris 1924

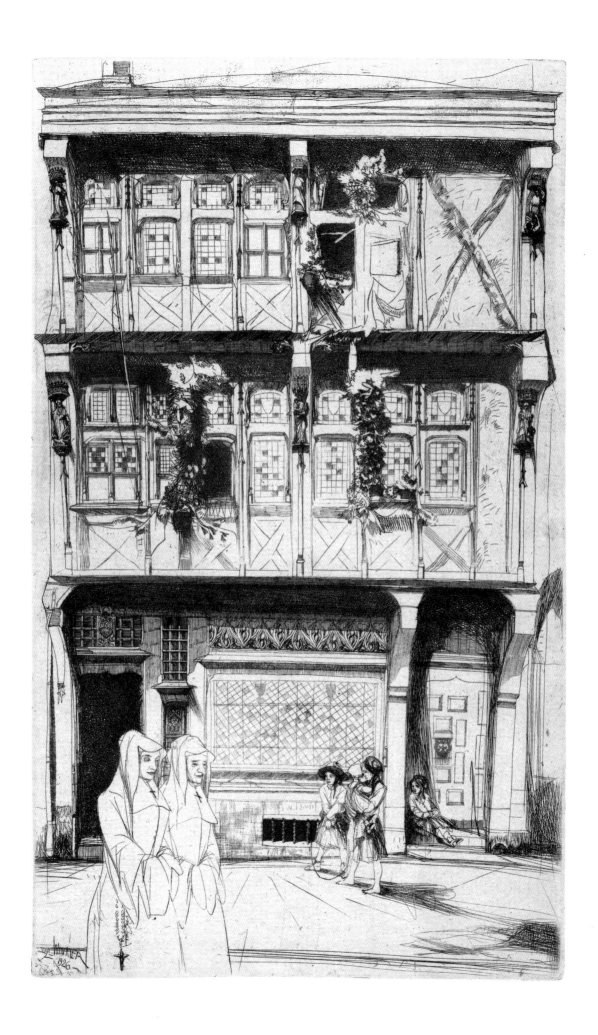

9. *To my friend John W. Winkler, master of us all.*
   John Taylor Arms, presentation print inscription, 1943

In 1935 the California Pacific International Exposition in San Diego borrowed prints of *Awnings and Balconies* and *Fisherman's Home* from the Los Angeles Public Library for exhibition in its southwest graphic arts section; on page 19, the catalogue listed artist John W. Winkler as "deceased." In view of the fact that Winks showed his Rouen etching *La Maison des Saintes* at the Chicago Society's April exhibition and issued *Chinese Card Players* (the finest of his large format Chinatown etchings) through the California Society of Etchers in San Francisco, this announcement of Winks' demise illustrated little other than the ignorance of the exposition's staff. But the error contained an inadvertent truth.

As the direct manifestation of his artistic disintegration, Winks' reputation was plagued by contradictions and disarray after his return to the West Coast in 1928. Until 1932, when he and Nora separated, Winks had pursued deliberate strategies for maintaining his public stature, primarily circulating improved or enlarged images from the San Francisco portfolio among new representatives in California.[1] Because his production of new plates had ground to a virtual standstill, this was his only realistic opportunity to generate income as the Depression deepened. After he took up solitary residence in Berkeley in June of 1932, first in modest quarters on Eunice Street and then as caretaker of Agnes Hoyle's decaying mansion at 1049 Keith Avenue, Winks withdrew entirely from the active management of his etching career. To the extent that he thought about the public at all, he studiously projected the image of a local eccentric, shielded in part from the intrusions of the outside world by his unorthodox zoologic coterie of pet skunks and the sluggish but

La Maison des Saintes
Rouen 1926

terrifying gila monster, Montezuma.[2] Critic Aline Kistler had remarked as early as 1930 that Winks was "something of a mystery,"[3] and by 1935 his impish refusal to correct the Exposition's catalogue error was in many ways the measure of his retreat.

In fact, the world to which he had returned bore little resemblance to the one he left in 1921. Winks sometimes excused his painfully slow production after 1930 by noting that the picturesque allure of San Francisco had vanished during his absence. Chinatown's romantic streets were now overrun by automobiles and Telegraph Hill had been mercilessly sanitized. Revealingly, Winks avoided any mention of those changes in the larger art world, which no doubt had more to do with his alienation than the advent of any upstart machine. The mercurial energy of the etching craze was entirely spent by the late 1920s. The American painter-etcher (to whose former prominence many allied graphic arts owed their establishment in the modern era) was in dark eclipse. Modernists now clamored for abstract imagery which repudiated literal renditions of the visual world. "Socially conscious" graphic moralists belittled the decorative products of the 1920s, demanding instead the frank and unsettling depiction of the social consequences of the Depression.[4] Openly excoriated for its former "preciocity" and sometimes accused of fostering a cult, etching itself was forced to take a democratic rank and file position among the graphic arts. And the print market had collapsed along with other speculative markets in the western world,[5] possibly the result of the wanton abuse of the limited edition. Whether Winks' manifest indifference to these momentous changes was a calculated protective posture or the very mirror of his disaffection, we do not know. Compounded by the strain of persistent emotional depression in the 1930s, it may have been foreseeable that his personal "mystery" should intensify in the face of far-reaching public rejection of those artistic values which two decades earlier had bestowed upon him his American identity.

If the world which had so captured Winks' imagination was gone, remembrance was nevertheless bright. In the decades following his return from Europe he turned to the deliberate exploitation of his own artistic past as the avenue to fulfillment of his resolute commitment to etching. In his studio, under the arching skylight on the second floor at Keith Avenue, Winks revisited the city of his youth, reworking the images of the San Francisco portfolio in the large format that characterized his work of the 1930s and 1940s. When anyone asked, Winks let it be known that he was laboring over "a monumental San Francisco set," but there was no binding principle among the images other than their common source in the plates created prior to 1921. Occasionally he mined the twenty-four English plates for another Thames image: *Police Boats* was reproduced in *Prints* in 1937, and won first prize at the California Society's annual exhibition in 1939.[6]

By degrees Winks mended, and in the late 1930s he was sufficiently buoyant to undertake the last of his genuine San Francisco adventures. He spent the better part of the years between 1937 and 1942 *plein air* etching on Fisherman's Wharf. Immersed in the small world of crab fishermen and ferryboats, Winks gave free reign to the imaginative whims which infuse these plates with lyric tendencies foreign to his earlier work. In former times, when all American etchers figuratively peered over his shoulder, he would not have taken the liberty to express the dark drama of *Storm Over the Pacific* or the delicate harmonies of *Flying Gulls*. His audience now limited to the citizenry of the San Francisco Bay area, who purchased the prints exclusively through the S. & G. Gump Company, Winks chose to delight the audience only to the extent that he pleased himself, leaving the greater fraction of the Fisherman's Wharf images to fend for themselves in the expanding clutter of his studio.

And so, as Winks succumbed to imaginative introversion, etching resumed its place as his private pastime. Reveling in the liberation of this development, on Fisherman's Wharf he was able once again to experience the freedom of his art and to etch for the sheer pleasure of the activity. Old friends such as John Taylor Arms and recent acquaintances such as Elizabeth Ginno (whom Winks would marry in 1949) contributed to the healing process and poured loving ingenuity into the often thankless task of sustaining affirmation for his etching during those intervals when Winks' artistic self-esteem ebbed. In the touch-and-go climate of his long depression, their devotion insured his survival, as Winks was quick to acknowledge in later years.

———————————

And then, commencing in 1936 and quite without analogue in his previous life, Winks found a companion to which he owed the renewal of his will to live. Of California's magnificent Sierra Nevada, Winks often said it was the *only* place where a human being could truly be alive. He had perhaps toured Yosemite with Nora in 1919, but after his return from Europe he took up the exploration of the pristine intimacies of the range. His fellow travelers were a handful of devotees of the pre-war Sierra Club,

William E. Colby prominent among them, whose benefactions included amenities such as campfire companionship and bedrock necessities such as transportation, for Winks, eschewing the symbol of the world to which he had returned was fully entrenched by then in his lifelong refusal to learn how to drive. In gratitude for the solace of the mountains, Winks embarked upon a secret project in which he somehow managed to blend the alpine longings of his Austrian heritage with his unquenchable enthusiasm for the American West. Relegating this work to the hours left over after the conclusion of his etching day, he referred to the laborious creation of some two hundred carved and painted boxes as his "hobby" or his "incidental work." For twenty years their production consumed his mind and his hand as the Sierra Nevada, and especially its stately trees, captured his heart. With tools he built specifically for the purpose, the boxes were handcarved from naturally seasoned chunks of Sierra timber that Winks and his cronies lugged back to Berkeley from the high country. He meticulously incised and oil painted them with those emblems of the range that recommend themselves for particular notice to the frequent visitor—many forms of mountain life from the lowly but inevitable ant to the raucous, freewheeling Clark's nutcracker.

Eventually Winks violated his own protocols by taking several months off from etching to work day and night in order to "finish" the Sierra project. Not surprisingly, it had acquired its own importance.[7] As Winks explained to Arms in 1948: "I believe this work is as perfect in its way as anything that has ever been made; by all odds, the most important thing, it has to my knowledge no counterpart anywhere, and I mean anywhere!"[8] Thus the "Sierra Nevadiana" boxes, not the etchings, had come to satisfy his craving for an expression completely unique to himself. Yet the consuming digression into the boxes was not responsible for his disaffection from etching. Well before he crafted the first chisel with which to carve them he had turned his back on the world of American graphic art.

Winks' alienation might be appreciated, if at all, from the perspective of his own tenacious belief that his worth as an artist would be judged in terms of etching he had not yet produced. Realizing his own worst fears, in the 1930s he came to see that his future would not yield those transcendent masterpieces which he believed would propel his name into the heavens of American printmaking. Of his several failures, perhaps the

Flying Gulls c.1941

most perplexing was his inability to comprehend the strength of the San Francisco portfolio, which had not only prompted the notoriety of the 1920s but also comprised the basis of the heightened admiration of succeeding generations. Nevertheless, after his return from Europe he was strangely deaf to the simple message of the critics of the new era.

Far from being drummed out of the American etching fraternity for failure to attain the unattainable, in everyone's estimation save his own Winks' position in the upper regions of the national printmaking meritocracy was secure—this in spite of the radical shift in artistic values and without regard for the lamentable pace of his production. In 1930, Bolton Brown echoed the refrain of the previous decade, ranking Winks with Whistler, Hayden, and Meryon.[9] In 1934, John Taylor Arms, then widely recognized as the "high priest of the etchers' cult," published his enduring tribute to Winks as the "master of line."[10] In 1937, Childe Reece, reviewing the American etching scene, referred to Winks without hesitation as "America's greatest etcher."[11] And in the same year, though he balked a bit, Winks gave in to Arms' gentle urgings and allowed himself to be elected an associate of the National Academy of Design.[12] Winks' detachment from these assessments stemmed in part from his frank disbelief that work by one as reckless with talent, as young and inexperienced as he had been, could possibly contain the highest expression of such a difficult art as etching. His bewilderment was genuine: from Winks' point of view his early work had assumed an incomprehensible life of its own.

---

1. Prior to Winkler's return to the Bay Area, Nora had conducted business on his behalf with Vickery, Atkins & Torrey. In 1930 this firm was supplanted by E. B. Courvoisier of San Francisco, which became his northern California representative. In 1929 Winkler had come to an arrangement with the book and print establishment of Roy V. Sowers, located on East Green Street in Pasadena, for consignment sales in southern California. He apparently avoided The Print Rooms, then located in Los Angeles, after his return. On the East Coast he continued with Frederick Keppel, though the absence of new plates limited their ability to promote his work. He also wrote to Doll & Richards in 1929, seeking to reopen the old relationship, but unaccountably failed to follow up on the warm response from that firm.

2. Winkler became notorious for his disregard of the common social courtesies, frequently refusing to answer his own door, for example, thus forcing his friends

Jetty at Fisherman's Wharf 1941

to the strenuous expedient of climbing through windows just to have a word with him. Once inside, sitting on the couch was risky, since "Monty" took his nap among its pillows. The American College Society of Print Collectors, which in 1940 presented its members with *Bermondsey Bridge* [sic], noted: "Winkler has been called unsocial, but he is an unaffected and charming host. If he lives alone in his big Spanish house with his pets (one a tamed Gila monster) and does not answer the telephone or the door bell or letters, it is only because he is so deeply concentrated on his work that these things are all trifling. But this makes it a rarer privilege to be counted as one of his friends."

3. Aline Kistler, "Etchings by Winkler on Exhibit," *San Francisco Chronicle*, January 19, 1930.

4. "Restricted output, fantastic prices, limited editions . . . These are the playthings of those who have money . . . There is bound to be, sometime, a bigger print world than this. The notion that art . . . good art . . . is necessarily aristocratic and not for the human being is worked for all it is worth in some quarters; but the movement of the age is, if slowly, still definitely, against it." Bolton Brown, "Prints and Their Makers," *Prints* 1 (November 1930): 20.

By 1936 the countermovement had found its sea legs. Spokesmen for the American Artists' Congress declared: "The one hundred prints here reproduced . . . may be characterized as 'socially conscious.' . . . More and more artists are . . . filling their pictures with their reactions to humanity about them, rather than with apples or flowers . . . [the public] no longer regards the print only as wall decoration, but as a form of contemporary expression. . . . The artist ceases to be an ornament of the pink-tea, a playboy companion of the dilettante patron, a remote hero with a famous name. . . . He prints his etchings, lithographs or woodblocks with hands which know ink and the rollers of wheels of his press. He works. He produces. He lives. . . . Lately the print has been perverted into a false, unhealthy, unnatural preciocity. . . . Fortunately, some artists have been forced, by the none too gentle jolts of the times, to open their eyes. . . . Prints are now being produced that portray the vital aspects of contemporary life. Editions are now unlimited. Prices are now low—not low enough yet—but even so more available to the huge new audience." Alex R. Stravenitz, Ralph M. Pearson and Harry Sternberg, introduction to *America Today: A Book of 100 Prints* (1936; reprint ed., *Graphic Works of the American Thirties*, New York: Da Capo Press, 1977), pp. 5–9.

5. "Speculation in etchings became very rampant during the boom of 1927. . . . During this boom speculators bought and sold so rapidly and repeatedly that the auction rooms became, for all the world, like miniature stock exchanges. At Sotheby's the number of print sales increased from the average half dozen a season to two a month, and the normal posse of phlegmatic dealers was surrounded by an *omnium gatherum* of semi-amateur speculators. . . . The

present slump in etchings is largely due to the artificial boom in prices that occurred some twelve years ago, by which many speculators made money, and through which many collectors have since suffered such heavy depreciation in the value of their collections that they have been obliged to suspend their purchases." Stanley Rowland, "The Decline of Etching," *Apollo* 32 (1940): 22.

6.   Edmilia Hodel, "Winkler Wins First Award in Etchers' Show," *San Francisco News*, October 21, 1939.

7.   Winkler's diary entry for Friday, September 26, 1951, reads: "Sierra Nevadiana completely finished. Starting from April 1st, all of my days were used to finish the work on the various boxes to get them ready for the exhibition in October. Never did I dream that it would require incessant labor during all these months to bring the work to a close, seeing that (with the exception of six of them) all were practically finished. . . . The work of finishing Sierra Nevadiana seemed endless, but now it's done and I made them as perfect as I possibly could. Begun in the early part of 1936 nearly sixteen years have elapsed since the first one was shaped into its form. What a time I had with some of them! And what ungodly hours they demanded of me. Only the gods know what will eventually become of them."

One hundred boxes and seventy conte crayon drawings of specific Sierra trees were first exhibited at the M. H. deYoung Memorial Museum in Golden Gate Park, October 20 through November 20, 1951. The California State Library, loyal to Winkler's work from the earliest days, exhibited Sierra Nevadiana in June of 1952. Winkler had dedicated the project to John Muir and William Colby, architects of the Sierra Club.

8.   Winkler to Arms, November 6, 1948, Winkler Archives.

9.   Brown, "Prints and Their Makers," p. 22.

10.   John T. Arms, "John W. Winkler, Master of Line," *Prints* 4 (January 1934): 1-13.

11.   Childe Reece, "Etching in the United States," *Prints* 8 (October 1937): 14.

12.   *National Academy Special Exhibition* (New York: National Academy of Design, 1939), Graphic Art Section, Work by Living Members: 69— *The Delicatessen Maker*, 70—*Mission Street Wharf, San Francisco*, 71— *Old Wharves of San Francisco*. Winkler was elected to full membership in 1940, but as late as 1949 the Academy was constrained to request in writing the "representative specimen" of his work which, under its constitution, was required for the "consummation" of his election. Eliot Clark to Winkler, November 10, 1949, Winkler Archives.

10. *Life's a chore for every bloke, down to the last and longest smoke.* Winkler to himself, n.d.

For nearly two decades, Winks single-mindedly pursued his idiosyncratic blend of daytime etching and nighttime carving, shutting out the voices of the larger art world, but he never successfully obliterated his longing for the life of America's brightest painter-etcher. Mercifully—and in outright defiance of many too many cigars—he lived to see the old reputation revived. By 1971, when the first of the modern exhibitions opened in a small gallery at 1817 Powell Street,[1] featuring images from the San Francisco portfolio that hadn't been seen in decades or that had never escaped his studio, it was only his unerring instinct for a dignified bearing that prevented him from an open gesture of gratitude before the dais of those capricious powers which had shaped his remarkable life. He had outlasted the anguish and he was finally wise enough to accept the praise.

The eight years between the exhibition on Powell Street and Winks' death on January 26, 1979, marked the initial phase of the modern John W. Winkler revival. Calling his work a "refreshing rarity" for its blend of "old-fashioned virtues" with the "uniqueness of personality and authenticity of feeling that extends the range of those sometimes tired traditional qualities," Thomas Albright's review of the 1971 exhibition gave early voice to the warm reaction of contemporary viewers.[2] In June of 1974 the Walton Gallery of San Francisco presented a major etching retrospective and that November the Achenbach Foundation displayed the full cross section of Winks' artistic endeavors at the Palace of the Legion of Honor.[3] Though fate so scheduled it that Winks would miss the opening of his one-man exhibition at the Brooklyn Museum in April of 1979, it had nevertheless been arranged for Gene Baro, the consulting

Self portrait c.1960
Ballpoint pen

The sands in my hourglass are running slowly out. I never dreamed that I would reach this age. Every human being is condemned to perish. I care nothing about it. The only thing is, I want to finish as much of my work as I can. All my life I was very lucky—I had a nice work room and nobody to bother me. But I liked people around me, too, people of a different category, people who would contradict me, that's what I wanted. Yes-people—you can have them around you by the millions. I can say "yes" myself. And you can laugh at my work all you want and I will join right in without being a hypocrite. And yet I have a certain respect for my work, naturally. I did the best I could, you know, but sometimes even the best that you can do isn't good enough. There was no such thing in my vocabulary as good enough. There never has been.

Winkler to Ron Wanglin, c.1975

curator, to meet Winks personally. The subtle force of Winks' perennial charm permeates Baro's fine catalogue essay, which opens with a simple statement that goes to the heart of the matter. "For Winkler," Baro said, "artistic activity was allied to a natural exuberance, a joy of life, an homage to the beauty of and interest in the physical world and to the rich complexity of culture. Whatever the medium, Winkler's art was rooted in his experience, a direct reaction to what moved him, amused him, delighted him. The impulse behind it was to share . . . the essential quality of what he had seen and felt."[4]

The qualities that were natural and inherent in Winks had rendered fickle service over the eight decades of their indenture. In the earliest days they had made of Vienna an intolerable prison. In the 1910s and 1920s they had made of John Winkler America's painter-etcher par excellence, for it was the expression of personality—the artist's "autograph"—which comprised the hallmark of the painter-etcher's art. Many artists had loved San Francisco, but no one had inscribed a personal reaction so deeply into every aspect of the fabulous seaport. And when etching no longer answered the impulse for creative expression and Winks moved on to other fields, the single principle of art as the direct expression of personality emanated from the unique products of his mature years. It was John Winkler's personality, after all, that gave his work its enduring character.

We do not know if anyone in Vienna ever realized what had become of the incorrigible youngster who ran away from the ancient townhouse in the shadow of Saint Stephens. In the mid-1970s, when Winks and Elizabeth took their much deserved vacation to western Europe, Winks happily revisited the Latin Quarter but could not be coaxed much further east. Though some bitterness remained, Vienna had long since become irrelevant, for through his work he had achieved the personal vindication it had withheld. If, toward the end, one put the proposition in terms of "artistic greatness," Winks' old doubts would rouse themselves and lumber dutifully to the fore, but underneath it all Winks understood very well that his artistic legacy was as impressive as it was unique.

Thus the pleasure of success was intense for him, and his last decade accorded him fulfillment precisely because in the revival of interest in his art lay a straightforward affirmation of his own being. His closer friends were heartened to observe that it pleased Winks beyond measure when persons everywhere not only valued but spontaneously

Self-portrait c.1917

enjoyed the varied products of his artistic lifetime, most notable among them those bright images of an engaging city which, like the artist, now belong to our history.

---

1. Etchings by John W. Winkler, November 14-28, 1971, presented by Marci Thomas at 1817 Powell Street, San Francisco, Calif.

2. Thomas Albright, "Winkler's Refreshing S.F. Etchings," *San Francisco Chronicle*, December 6, 1971.

3. John W. Winkler Retrospective, San Francisco Etchings 1912–1967, June 1–26, 1974, Walton Galleries, 575 Sutter Street, San Francisco; Etchings, Drawings, and Boxes by John W. Winkler, November 16–December 15, 1974, Achenbach Foundation for Graphic Arts, California Palace of the Legion of Honor, San Francisco, curated by Fenton Kastner with catalogue by William B. and Ida Mae DuBois.

4. Gene Baro, "John W. Winkler: Drawings, Prints, Boxes" (New York: The Brooklyn Museum, 1979), p. 7. At the time, Baro was consulting curator for the Brooklyn Museum and somewhat later took on the additional role of adjunct curator of contemporary art for the Carnegie Institute. Baro was also a former director of the Corcoran Gallery.

EPILOGUE. . . . perhaps most of all, he was a consummate artist, and my love of and belief in the extraordinary quality of his work has continued to grow since I first saw it more than thirty years ago.

I first met John Winkler in the early sixties when he was living in the big Palladio-style home known affectionately to family and friends as the "plaster palace." The huge living quarters were downstairs but the crude kitchen had never been finished off and there was no heat except what the fireplaces provided. Upstairs was a really grand space, with a great skylight and a balcony which was inhabited by Winks' skunks. A large portion of that second floor was Winks' work space—his studio. He had so much room that he could just shove something aside if he didn't want to move it.

The next time I saw him was about eight months later at a Christmas gathering. The plaster palace was warm, with hearty blazes in the fireplaces, and the company was interesting. I recall meeting Dr. Catherine Bishop, whom Winks claimed was the codiscoverer of Vitamin E, and also Oscar Maurer, then ninety-one years young and famous for his photographs of the 1906 earthquake devastation in San Francisco. Dave Bohn was there, as was Eleonore Ginno (Elizabeth Winkler's sister), and Moonok Sunwoo managed to photograph the oldest (Oscar) and youngest (our six-month-old daughter) in attendance. Later, as all of us were getting ready to depart, Elizabeth casually laid some of Winks' French work on a large round table in the living room. Although Winks immediately scolded "Put those things away," Elizabeth ignored the command. But the Paris pen-and-ink sketches made an indelible impression on me. I was captivated by the beautiful fluidity and sparsity of line. As I looked at them, I said to him, "I feel as though my eye has been cheated." I knew I had heard the name John Winkler, somewhere in the art world, yet had not read of any exhibits in museums or galleries, at least not in my

Maria Theresa Thomas
1966. Pencil

time. (As to the way in which Elizabeth displayed the work, in retrospect I realized that this scenario was part of the Winklers' staging, especially if they thought they had an audience. In truth, Winks was proud of his work and very pleased to see people enjoying it. In all of the years that followed I never saw him tire of receiving intelligent appreciation of his efforts.)

It was probably in the late sixties that the Winkler family started to talk about getting Winks' work before the public again. Since the etchings had not been exhibited in twenty years there had been little or no income from them, although Winks certainly did not make art with an eye to sales. His artistic activity was allied to his joy of life and was homage to his love of the natural world. But Winks was rather negative about the possibility of showing his work again after all those years. He seemed convinced that people would not understand what they were looking at and that it would not sell. There was also some difficulty in getting him past the idea of the old numbers—for example, the price that had probably been written in during the 1920s. It was now 1971 but he thought fifteen dollars would be just fine. (Of course, it must be remembered that Winks was not in touch with prices on anything. I do not think he knew what a loaf of bread cost.)

Nevertheless, I proposed that there be a showing of his work in San Francisco, for which my good friends Virginia Anawalt and Marianne Myers (interior designers) would make available to me a small but exquisite space at 1817 Powell Street. Eventually, with Elizabeth's help, I chose for the walls views of Chinatown, Fisherman's Wharf, and some of the very early historic views of San Francisco. Suites of the Paris and London drawings and etchings would be viewed on a big conference table. As we considered choices from some three hundred items, Winks pretended not to be interested in the proceedings. He would walk in and grumble, and make critical comments about some of the prints, but he was obviously pleased that we were going over his work with a show in mind.

When the big day arrived, November 14, 1971, Winks was in fine form. He was charmed by the beauty and intimacy of the gallery and many of his old friends were present, including Leon Abrams (his art school roommate) and wife Suzanne, Imogen Cunningham, Eleonore Ginno, and Elsa Gerstel (who bought the first print—*Ross Alley*). A few days after the opening a call came from Elizabeth Baldwin, who had not seen Winks since their days at the San Francisco Institute of Art, some fifty-five years earlier. She had noticed Thomas Albright's review in the *Chronicle* and wanted to meet with Winks. This was arranged and the extraordinary visit took place at the gallery.

The Powell Street exhibit—a long-overdue tribute after the "disappearance" of Winks' work for more than two decades—created a lot of momentum. Subsequently the work was shown at the Winkler studio in 1972 and 1973, and in 1974 at the Walton Gallery (then on Sutter Street) and at the Palace of the Legion of Honor, where Fenton Kastner mounted a major retrospective with the assistance of lifelong friend William DuBois, who had for some years been wading through the chaos of Winks' papers to produce a chronology for the prints and then a catalogue for the Legion exhibit. And concurrent with the Legion show I opened a gallery at 560 Sutter Street with many of the San Francisco etchings, and the first-night crush was so great that we lodged Winks in a side room until the huge crowd thinned down.

As it turned out, at that time Winks had less than five years left to him but I know he thoroughly enjoyed the resurgence of his reputation. For anyone who knew and loved Winks, it was always very special to take the time to enter his world—from the beautiful books he cherished to the lively tales of Montezuma and the skunks, or the marvelous tale of the day his canned peaches blew up and covered the kitchen ceiling at the plaster palace. Winks was witty, a bit of a rascal, and one of the dearest humans I will ever know. The focus exhibited in his work carried over to his relationships with friends. When he talked with you there was total concentration—he talked *with* you and he listened carefully to your responses. But perhaps most of all, he was a consummate artist, and my love of and belief in the extraordinary quality of his work has continued to grow since I first saw it more than thirty years ago. Happily, it is still possible to enter the rich and gently humorous world of John Winkler through his etchings and drawings. *Marci Thomas, Berkeley*

REMINISCENCE. . . . one of his high Sierra trips. Briefly put, he ran out of tobacco and forced himself to puff on ground-up pine needles.

For me, an especially enduring memory of John Winkler has been the wonderful sense of humor, laced as it was with a substantial dose of irreverence. This humor was present not only face to face but surfaced throughout his work, especially in the early drawings and the Christmas-card etchings, and occasionally he carved it in three dimensions during the years of the Sierra Nevadiana box project, an opus which will be described below in some detail. Thus, always the humor, whether in conversation, on paper, or carved in wood. And regarding the latter, I love to call to mind the 1943 "tobacco" box, dimensioned (roughly) at eight-by-seven-by-eight inches with a hinged lid of four panels carrying words to match the painted scene on the side below. Of the four panels I have two favorites: the old Austrian sitting in his chair, pipe in hand, calling to his dog—"Dachshund, Pipe / A Krügel Beer / Alte come and light sie mir"; and then the scene of five Greek philosophers standing near the Parthenon with a poem that is vintage Winks, including the spelling—"Still wiser would / They've been theese blokes / Could they have passed / Around some smokes."

For the most part Winks lived as he preached. He really did believe (for a time, at any rate) that smoking conveyed an extra dose of sagacity, especially pipesmoking, with which he was obsessed for years. So much so that by the mid-1940s he had a collection of some three hundred Prince Albert tobacco tins stacked neatly in rows floor to ceiling in his studio. Yes, they did fall over once, but of course he restacked. Eventually the tins were given away for the metal including the one that contained the money stash. Although I think the best story on Winks' pipe-smoking obsession came out of one of his high Sierra trips. Briefly put, he ran out

Winkler at his studio
by Dave Bohn 1970

of tobacco and forced himself to puff on ground-up pine needles. Stories on top of stories, but I am getting ahead of myself. I better start from the beginning.

I first met John and Elizabeth Winkler at the so-called "plaster palace" at 1049 Keith Avenue, Berkeley, in December of 1962. The occasion was a dinner party and I had been invited because one of my mountaineering friends, Moonok Sunwoo, wanted me to meet this uncharacterizable couple. On ringing the bell, the doors—two gigantic carved redwood panels—were opened by the master etcher himself, who, bowing low with a sweep of the arm ushered me into the mammoth living room. A few seconds later, having completed a quick visual survey of the unusual space, I said to Winkler, "My god, what a joint." Some fifteen years later, when he was approaching a ninth decade, Winks was still reminding me of that utterance. I think the irreverence of the comment grabbed him, and I also think he was immediately aware of the fact that he could not buffalo me, a favorite trick with so many of his new acquaintances. Such matters apparently paved the way to an enduring friendship which, later on, included hours of taping, many discussions of the high Sierra and especially *trees*, and occasional sessions of portrait photography, for which Winks always required "assurance" that the camera held no film. Assurance granted, he would then endlessly pose without being asked, especially if he had pipe to hand.

Of course, I knew Winks only through his last seventeen years and by then he had mellowed. The earlier volatility, combining huge mood swings and wild outbursts of temper, suggests that attainment of a ninth decade was a remarkable achievement. Credit for that achievement does not go to Winks, however, but to Elizabeth Ginno Winkler, who put up with him and kept him going for more than forty-five years. Had she not done so, John Winkler would almost certainly have voluntarily departed this vale of tears long before age almost-ninety.

Elizabeth deGébele Ginno was born in July of 1907 in London. Her father was a naturalized U.S. citizen and the travel occasion was a visit to his relatives. Elizabeth grew up in Berkeley, went through the elementary grades at Oxford School, then for three and a half years attended the Cora L. Williams Institute for Creative Education in north Berkeley, with an emphasis on art. But Cora Williams' institute was not "scholarly" enough to suit Elizabeth's parents so they packed her onward for three years at Miss Randolph's School, also in Berkeley, and then came a scholarship to Mills College where she majored in art and drama. In 1928, Elizabeth married Carol Aronovici and had two children, John and daughter Carol. (In keeping with Elizabeth's involvement in staged drama, the Aronovicis founded Stagecraft Studios, still in existence at 1854 Alcatraz Avenue, Berkeley.) The marriage ended in divorce in 1933. By then Elizabeth was living on Rose Street, not far from Winks' Eunice Street quarters, a bachelor's domestic chaos that included a kitchen so indescribably filthy and messy that he almost never bothered to eat.

Meanwhile, Elizabeth's mother (who also lived nearby) had noticed "this foreign-looking gentleman" wearing spats and carrying a fancy cane running for the streetcar. The gentleman was Winks, of course, and through one of his next door neighbors he and Elizabeth were eventually introduced. Shortly thereafter Elizabeth began her attempts at making order in the execrable kitchen, plus washing clothes, in exchange for drawing lessons. Given Winks' irascible and overly dramatic temperament, given that Nora was now also living in Berkeley (and still playing chamber music with Winks), and given that Elizabeth was struggling to bring up two children, the situation that developed was not a simple one. Nevertheless, regarding those first months of acquaintance with him, Elizabeth recalls ". . . sitting in a canvas chair in John Winkler's messy kitchen, looking out of a leaf-shaded window. Out there I imagined I saw a long path. That path seemed to be for me to follow. I had my baby with me, asleep in the dining room, and the easel was set up for drawing lessons. I was at the broken end of my marriage and Winks was at a crossroad of his own. So I started on the path I had seen beyond the kitchen window."

Two years later, in 1935, Winks heard grapevine that his Eunice Street landlady had been accused of arson in Mill Valley and at the same time learned that San Francisco attorney Agnes Hoyle needed a caretaker for her house at 1049 Keith Avenue. Winks was startled, to say the least, at even the remotest possibility that his archives might go up in smoke and therefore needed little urging to move. This monumental effort included the etching press he had carted from Paris, oceans of antique printing paper, all of his plates, all of his prints, an enormous and extremely eclectic library, assorted antique bric-a-brac and, not least, dozens of cacti-filled pots (Winks was a fanatical gardener). But as Elizabeth recounts: "There was more than enough room for everything in that crazy, imitation

'Italian Villa.' It was huge. It had a thirty-by-thirty-foot upstairs studio with an enormous circular skylight, it had balconies ideal for the cactus collection, it had a sunken bath so big it took one hour to fill, it had two fireplaces (but no furnace) and a huge living room, and it even had a 'secret' room." Certain of the eccentricities Winks covered over with muslin and gunny sacking—for example, the studio murals and the *putti* flowing out of ceiling corners. However, as Nora said to him at the time, "Now you have your plaster palace." And so, 1049 Keith Avenue became home and workplace for some twenty-eight years. (The house was unusual, to say the least. It was built by Paul Beygrau and his wife during the years 1925–1930, and they named it "Villa Florival" or "flower temple." Much of the material that went into the building was packed up the hill by Beygrau himself. He and his wife handtooled the various redwood doors and she painted the studio murals, which represented cherished memories—her birthplace in Alsace, his father's home in England, and plants, ferns and trees native to California. But as the depression came on Beygrau lost his job, sank into debt, and the Beygraus subsequently lost their "little castle" to foreclosure.)

During the years at 1049, Winks encountered enormous frustration with his work and suffered often from what Elizabeth has characterized as "deep depression." Both of them worried endlessly about making ends meet, but especially Elizabeth who can, even this many years later, remember a ten-cent streetcar fare as spendthrift in going to market for a bag of potatoes. For his part, Winks had essentially cut himself off from his print market before returning from Paris and he never personally attempted to re-establish that market to any extent. Thus, to offset the disastrous economics of their situation Elizabeth worked at a number of jobs, culminating in a twenty-six year stint on the U.C. Berkeley campus as draftswoman and illustrator for the engineering department, 1945 until retirement in 1971.

But in spite of the incessant pressures to make ends meet, Elizabeth was managing to develop into an artist in her own right, eventually succeeding in synthesizing her humor with a wonderful sense of design, combining a technical facility nurtured in the drawing lessons Winks gave her, and subsequently in painting, drawing, and lithography classes at California College of Arts and Crafts, the San Francisco Institute of Art, and U.C. Berkeley. In the mid-1930s she did a set of thirty-two hand-colored flower etchings which are superb. In the late 1930s she did some outstanding oil paintings, pastels, and other exhibit

Winkler etching
by Elizabeth Winkler c.1938
Black conte crayon

pieces including Indian scenes for the National Park Service, all of these part of the WPA museum project at Berkeley. During the Golden Gate International Exposition 1939–1940 she demonstrated etching at the Treasure Island Fine Arts Palace and drew and painted the costumes of foreign participants on a daily basis. And in 1940 Elizabeth joined the California Society of Etchers—now the California Society of Printmakers—and was active in the organization for more than forty years, often in the role of secretary, which required of her almost endless correspondence. Winks was jealous of the time she spent on behalf of the Society but she felt the contacts she provided him with other artists was good for him. The jealousy moderated, however, when the Society bestowed honorary membership on Winks. Later on, Elizabeth exhibited in group and one-person shows at the American Graphic Society and National Academy of Design in New York, the Legion of Honor, the De Young, the Chicago Art Institute, and the Oakland Museum, among others.

As Elizabeth worked to help support herself and her children and Winks, he hid out in his plaster palace, alternating between depression and living the exalted (but extremely reclusive) life of an *artist*. Having already cut himself off from the "outside" world of etching, he had by now virtually eliminated the rest of the world too, rarely getting himself off the property to see anyone and on many occasions refusing to answer the doorknocker, sometimes even when he knew it was Elizabeth, who was still living on Rose Street though constantly checking in at Keith Avenue to make sure Winks was eating, working, and surviving. To suggest, therefore, that the twenty-eight-plus years at Keith were "difficult" ones would be putting it mildly. As noted earlier, Winks was irascible. He was also extremely volatile, such that one never knew what tiny miscue might cause an explosion. These attributes mixed with Elizabeth's willfulness resulted in on-again off-again turmoil, a turmoil that not infrequently reached the level of items thrown and items smashed. Nevertheless, in spite of the rather wild personality mix the long-range concept remained intact and *would* remain intact for the rest of Winks' life: Elizabeth firmly believed, almost religiously so, in Winks' work, and wanted to do anything in her power to make sure his creativity had reign. And while Winks probably did not believe in his own work quite as fiercely as did Elizabeth, in his own eyes he was the pure artist—first, last, and especially foremost.

Between and among the bouts of depression, lack of confidence, fear, and extreme self-criticism, Wink nevertheless spent the years at the plaster palace working and re-working the old plates and occasionally producing new ones. By about 1940, however, he was focusing the creative energy on packtrips to the Sierra Nevada, out of which came the superb conte crayon tree drawings, a number of mountain etchings, and especially the boxes. In fact, the boxes became not just passion but consuming passion; when the apparently obligatory weekday etching hours were out of the way, when dinner (if any) was out of the way and the hour was *finally* late and there would be no distractions, Winks would descend to the basement and work on his boxes through the night and into the wee hours of the morning. For twenty years he maintained this regimen, eventually producing some 230 of these exquisite objects.

Winks said on a number of occasions, "I only live when I am in the mountains." From the mid-1930s until the beginning of the war Winks went to the high Sierra whenever he could—to draw the trees, to etch the mountains, and to collect dead-tree rootwood for what became the inestimable box project. For the Sierra Nevadiana boxes he especially favored whitebark pine, and the Sierra juniper and Tamarack pine—Pinus albicaulis, Juniperus occidentalis, and Pinus contorta—but in the course of the twenty-year project he also utilized the wood of some seven other mountain trees. Using a folding brush saw and a carpenter's handsaw, root pieces were collected and transported to Berkeley by car, with Winks draped around and amongst the large chunks on the long drives back. Subsequent shaping, gouging, and carving were achieved by use of hand tools; a saw for blocking out, rasp and chisel and file for shaping, a very small homemade gouge for removing excess from inside lid and body, calipers for symmetry, and knife for carving and finishing. The basic shape was rectangular, with tapered lid and topknot, and feet—the entire item formed out of a single piece of wood. Size varied from miniature to large, lids were hinged with brass, and surfaces were sealed with white shellac *only*, a point consistently made by Winks because the high resin content of the material would have prevented varnish from drying. Some of the boxes were left plain, but many of them were beautifully scribed with Sierra Nevada scenes including mountains, lakes, trees, and animals. In some cases, a motif was chosen—such as butterflies, bees, a flower, ants—and repeated across the surfaces of body and lid. And finally, with incredible delicacy, the pictorial elements were painted within the scribed outline with Winsor & Newton opaque oil colors. The boxes were rarely

shaped and carved and then decorated in the same year, in some instances decoration occurring more than a decade after the production.

And it simply did not matter to Winks how many weeks or months or even years he lavished on any particular piece. The so-called "parquet" box, for example, was constructed from 130 joined pieces outside and 281 joined pieces inside, and occupied him on and off from 1936 to 1943. But for tenacity and obsession perhaps the "bomb" box—so named for its shape—takes the cake. From Winks' box log, this undated entry: "This piece of wood was partly shaped, when the worm holes became more numerous as the work progressed. It was finally abandoned and thrown away! About 3 months later I came across it again and decided not to let it lick me. In the end I was forced to make over 130 dowels of the same wood of different sizes, drill the holes and fit each one in. The wood comes from Humphrey's Basin. Wood: Tamarack. Made in 1928. Decor. 1942."

Once the boxes are seen, consuming passion and long-range commitment are readily understood. As a body of work, as an extraordinary statement of love of and participation with subject matter, the boxes are every square millimeter the equivalent of the etchings and not a whit short of that. And the basement workspace out of which came this remarkable project? It perhaps resembled a monastic cell, given size and location. Brick-on-dirt floor was surrounded on two sides by a low retaining wall and the dimension of the rectangle was about eight-by-seven feet, which meant Winks had to be careful not to smash his elbow on backstroke when using the handsaw. Storage shelves floor to ceiling on two sides plus worktable space were an utter chaos of wood, tools, and boxes in various stages, the whole of it illuminated by a solitary bulb underneath a steel reflector hanging from a ceiling cord.

Winks was fond of quotes. One of his favorites was taken from Goethe, or so he said. He wrote it out longhand, mounted it on a card and propped it on his worktable where it sat for about thirty years: "What you can do, or dream you can . . . Begin it! Only engage, and then the mind grows heated—Begin, and then the work will be completed!" Winks spent twenty years on the boxes. The last decorations were added in 1957, at which point he decided he had exhausted the possibilities of the basic shape and thus he considered the project complete.

On October 26, 1948, Winks and Nora were divorced, some twenty years after the separation. The proceedings were handled by Agnes Hoyle, and

Echo Lake: Sierra Juniper
1953. Carbon pencil

Kennedy Meadows: Sierra Juniper
1945. Carbon pencil

Echo Lake: Sierra Juniper
1953. Carbon pencil

according to his diary Winks was quite devastated by the courtroom experience, especially since Nora also attended the session. The financial agreement required Winks to pay Nora $1400 at the rate of $50 a month. Winks and Elizabeth then married in December of 1949 and she moved permanently to 1049 Keith Avenue.

If the decade of the 1940s occasionally saw Elizabeth standing in line for free carrots and potatoes, the 1950s were just a little bit kinder financially to the Winklers. Several major San Francisco collectors were making occasional purchases from Winks, there were a number of Bay area exhibits with attendant sales (also an exhibit in 1955 in Arnhem, Holland, of more than fifty etchings but with no sales allowed), and Winks devised a plan with Elizabeth's sister, Eleonore Ginno, whereby he gardened for her weekly and eventually qualified himself for the minimum Social Security benefit. So the months and years lurched onward at 1049 Keith, with Elizabeth as always trying to hold things together. Not easy, given Winks' wild mood swings, his eccentric working hours, the almost constant shortage of money, the social isolation (on all too many weekends Winks and Elizabeth were rattling around the house together getting under each other's feet), and the deterioration of the plaster palace. For in spite of proud written statements to the contrary, via correspondence between the Beygraus and Agnes Hoyle, the house was poorly built. The cement-over-wood construction did not work well, the outside plaster decorations were constantly falling off, and once when Elizabeth opened the front door she saw that the pillars had fallen over. There were endless leaks and the building was creeping downhill.

Fortunately for Winks and Elizabeth, as the 1950s drew to a close Agnes Hoyle would not sell them 1049 Keith Avenue, so they found a place in El Cerrito and the move was made in 1964, of course including the two skunks. Although Winks could not carry away his fruit trees and vegetable garden and terraced backyard, he *could* lug the prized cacti and start all over. Which is exactly what he did. The etching was more or less finished other than occasional fine-tuning, the box project was complete, but the gardening would go on. By now in his mid-seventies, Winks labored mightily in the rock and dirt piles and no visit to him during the late 1960s and early 1970s was complete without the obligatory tour to see the latest retaining wall, the newest terrace, the most recently planted cacti, and the fruit trees. During his last few years Winks could no longer work outside, but by then the legacy of the garden was being carried forward by Elizabeth's son, John Aronovici. *Dave Bohn, Berkeley*

– 171 –

*Mounts Banner and
Ritter 1964*

Photograph by Leon Abrams, 1916. Writing to an acquaintance Morris Dallett c. 1950, Winkler characterizes this photograph as "... one of the finest portraits ever made of me during any period of my life." In the same letter, he went on to recall that it had been taken by his roommate Leon Abrams at their quarters in San Francisco—the Glencliff—at three *a.m.*, with a Graflex. (Winkler self-legend has it that Helene Zwicker, the two rascals' landlady, heard the flash powder explosion and then, of course, detected the smoke. Especially given the ungodly hour, she told them they had to leave but apparently never followed through on the peremptory order.) Dallett had then come up with a fine print, "... that you so successfully enlarged from a mere faded pinpoint of a film. How you managed to achieve this will always be shrouded in mystery for me. I know so little, in fact next to nothing, about the making of a photograph. It seems to me a very complicated and tricky medium."

Winkler is etching *At Leisure* here (see p. 184), and the reproduction is taken from Dallett's early print since the negative is apparently long gone. There is no other known early photographic image of Winkler biting a plate.

When Abrams took this superb early-morning composition, Winkler was on the verge of the breakthrough into some of his greatest Chinatown work (*Chowseller, Gingershop, The Delicatessen Maker, Quiet Corner,* for example), many of which were etched in 1917, also at the Glencliff. It is no surprise then, that Winkler treasured for the rest of his life what Abrams recorded. No artist could hope for more in a photographic portrait.

Photograph by Dorothea Lange, c.1918. During the 1930s and into the 1940s, Imogen Cunningham produced a number of portraits of Winkler, as Dorothea Lange had done much earlier. The contrast between the two sets is marked. In virtually all of the Lange photographs Winkler is bursting with enthusiasm or, at least, smiling. In virtually all of the Cunningham photographs, however, he appears moody and brooding.

In the 1950s, Cunningham was asked by Elizabeth Winkler, who was participating in a taped three-way conversation, "Why was Winks never laughing in any of your pictures?" The first part of the answer was, "Because I don't take laughing people." And Cunningham's interest, via the photographic portrait, in Winkler's "bitterness" (see p. 93, note 7) comes up later in the same conversation as she describes his dark moods as ". . . black as the burnt California hills."

Indeed, Cunningham's metaphor is a good one but also extremely selective. The dark moods, for the most part, came upon Winkler when he was alone in confrontation with his work. But when he was willing to be photographed—which was most of the time—he was *invariably* sunny and mellow and the humor almost always showed in the portrait. Thus, of all those who photographed Winkler down through the years, only Cunningham consistently selected the dark side for portrayal.

The Heintzelman table, c.1925, Paris. Arthur W. and Katherine
Heintzelman arrived in Paris about mid-1921, thus preceding the Winklers
by only a few months. The Heintzelmans' hotel apartment, at 4 sq.
Desnouettes, rather quickly became an anchorage for Winkler. He went to
dinner there often, with or without Nora, and Heintzelman reciprocated
by visiting the Winklers' dinner table and salon, at 5 rue Corneille, also
on many occasions. With the addition of John Taylor Arms and wife
Dorothy, "this trio of American junior etchers" became an enclave and
took every opportunity to be together.

   We do not know who made the photograph, but fortunately two
contact prints (22.5 × 16.8 cm) have survived in the Winkler Archives,
one of them truly superb. As to the lineup, Arthur Heintzelman is at the
right, Winkler at left, and John Taylor Arms at center. Nonsensical left-to-
right documentation typed under the print has confused identification of
the ladies, except for Nora Winkler who sits at Arms' left. Presumably,
Penelope Noyes (Dorothy Noyes Arms' aunt?) is front left, Katherine
Heintzelman is next, and Dorothy Arms sits forward at the right side.

Photograph by Cedric Wright, c.1936. Here is Winkler in the basement of 1049 Keith Avenue, Berkeley, with one of his beloved "Sierra Nevadiana" boxes in the vise and two others on the workbench. Rasps, chisels, gouger, and hand drill are in evidence but, more importantly, one can see immediately the inevitable extraordinary clutter. A slightly expanded description of this subterranean workspace is given on page 167.

In retrospect, it would have been appropriate if Cedric Wright had included in the photograph a chunk of Sierra rootwood and the solitary bulb hanging from the ceiling cord. But Wright's back was already against the wall, quite literally, in producing the only visual record we have of Winkler in the process of creating one of his two hundred-plus Sierra Nevadiana masterpieces.

Photograph by Dave Bohn, January 21, 1973. During his final years Winkler did no real printing. Rather, he fussed endlessly with his plates, occasionally sprucing up a line here or there but mostly inking and wiping. Every so often he would put a copper on his press and pull an impression, but the result was never (by then) up to his nearly impossible standard. However, these sessions were almost certainly his way of staying in touch with old friends.

The occasion here was a very quiet Sunday afternoon and there had not been, nor would there be, any conversation. In fact, there was not even awareness of camera on Winkler's part, a very rare circumstance because he loved to strike heroic poses for the photographer. But just the old friends this time and camera didn't matter.

And then, some weeks later, Winkler decided the photograph—as one of only two or three ever taken of him on press—was more than up to par and could he have a print? Indeed, yes he could.

Library Site c.1915

AFTERWORD. No other artist contributed so much of himself to a city whose narrative was that of vicissitude and change.

There is great romance attached to the history of San Francisco and part of that romance would have disappeared had it not been for John W. Winkler, who played such an important role in recording our city's history. No other artist contributed so much of himself to a city whose narrative was that of vicissitude and change. From the fifty-year span of work, his legacy made it possible for present and future generations to study San Francisco's once-familiar spots and well-known forms and places that have faded from view.

I am one of those "future generations" that became enamored of an artist who, with his soaring mind and flexible thought, was able to etch on copper plates the very soul of San Francisco. With patience and tenacity he climbed Telegraph Hill to sketch the life styles of the Irish and Italians. His walks through Chinatown, once referred to as "a ward of Canton set down in the most valuable business property in the city," produced his best known works, now so important to the historian, the illustrator, and the antiquarian. His stupendous depictions of man and ships on the waterfront continue to remind us of excitement past—as compared to our lifeless and colorless port of today.

Each of the Winkler etchings in the collection of the San Francisco Public Library was acquired with one thought in mind: was there a photograph in the collection that pictured the same idea? If the answer was no, then another silent thank you went out to a man who left a superb pictorial legacy. *Gladys Hansen, San Francisco*

At Leisure 1916

1894   July 31: Born Vienna

1910   Drops out of Schotten (?) *gymnasium*, leaves for the United States. Changes name to John William Winkler on forged passport

1911   Reaches Giltner, Nebraska

1912   November: Enrolls at San Francisco Institute of Art

1913   Produces first etchings, early in the year

1914   March: Produces first *plein air* etching, *Building City Hall*

1915   May: Exhibits paintings, pen and ink drawings, and etchings at SFIA student exhibition. Wins SFIA's first etching prize and "life scholarship"
        Early summer: Exhibits small collection from the *Views of San Francisco* portfolio at San Francisco Art Association's "First Exhibit of Painting and Sculpture," Golden Gate Park Memorial Museum
        December: Exhibits *Library Site* and *Building City Hall* at California Society of Etchers annual and becomes member

1916   Obtains position as gas lamplighter for San Francisco
        Spring: First known publication of any Chinatown image, *Dark Alley*, in SFIA's summer school catalogue

1917   March: Exhibits nationally at American Institute of Graphic Arts, N.Y., with *At Leisure, Freighting*, and *Irmgard*

1918   From late 1916 to early in this year etches many of his finest Chinatown plates, including *The Delicatessen Maker, Chowseller, Gingershop, Quiet Corner*, and *Corner Fruitstand*
        March: Exhibits with Chicago Society of Etchers and wins one of their four annual Logan prizes
        November: Exhibits five Chinatown images with Brooklyn Society of Etchers
        Fall: Marries Nora Crowe

1919   February: First dealer representation and first one-man show, at E.H. Furman's The Print Rooms, San Francisco
        March: Wins second CSE Logan prize

1920   January: Wins third CSE Logan prize
        Spring: Representation by Doll & Richards, Boston
        Fall: Representation by Carl Smalley, McPherson, Kansas. Exhibits at Doll & Richards, Concord (Mass.) Art Association, Brooklyn Society of Etchers, and Museum of History, Science and Art in Los Angeles (December), his first one-man exhibit in southern California
        November 11: Characterized as "artist laureate of San Francisco" by Boston *Evening Transcript*

1921   Winter-Spring: Exhibits at CSE (Chicago), the Los Angeles Print Makers second international, and J.S. Bradstreet of Minneapolis
May 16: Issued certificate of naturalization
July: Major retrospective and "farewell" exhibition at The Print Rooms, San Francisco
August: Leaves for Paris. Meets with Bertha Jaques in Chicago and concludes arrangements for representation with Frederick Keppel in New York

1921-1928   Paris: In addition to the French etchings, produces a London "set" from the banks of the Thames and a series of pencil and pen and ink drawings

1924   January: Exhibits at Galeries Simonson, Paris
March: Exhibits at Guiot Galeries, Paris

1925   February: Exhibits at James Connell & Sons galleries, London

1926   Fall: Nora Winkler returns to the United States

1928   January: Returns to the United States

1929   May: Exhibits at Victoria and Albert Museum, London

1932   Produces 1000 prints of his *The Constitutional Convention* for the George Washington Memorial Association's portfolio, *The Bicentennial Pageant of George Washington.* Twenty etchers contributed, edited by John Taylor Arms

1935   "Discovers" the Sierra Nevada and begins to produce a series of mountain etchings, conte crayon drawings of trees, and carved rootwood boxes

1930-1940   Produces a series of large plates of San Francisco subject matter, concentrating especially on Fisherman's Wharf. Re-establishes association with California Society of Etchers as etcher/judge

1949   December: Marries Elizabeth Ginno

1951   October: Carved boxes and conte crayon drawings exhibited at M.H. deYoung Memorial Museum in Golden Gate Park, San Francisco

1955   May: Exhibits at Kunstzaal Binsbergen, Arnhem, Holland

1957   March: Carved boxes and French drawings exhibited at California State Library, Sacramento

1971   November: Exhibits etchings and drawings at 1817 Powell Street gallery, San Francisco. Curated by Marci Thomas

1974   June: Retrospective at Walton Galleries, San Francisco
November: Etchings, drawings, and carved boxes exhibited at California Palace of the Legion of Honor, San Francisco

1979   January 26: Dies at El Cerrito, California
April: Retrospective at Brooklyn Museum, with catalogue essay by Gene Baro

Vegetable Wagon 1916

Plates are reproduced at 100% of the original unless otherwise indicated.

Buffallos. *J.J. Paris*   *Heurdein*

John W. Winkler's book was set in Trump by Words Worth of Santa Barbara. Production liaison by Terence Tumbale of DNP America; laser-scanned halftones by Bill Smith of Cal Central Press, Sacramento; biographical research, text and footnotes by Mary Millman; image research, essays, design and production by Dave Bohn. Two thousand copies were printed.

John·
William·
Winkler·

*Lake Tenaya: Glaciated Granite
and Sierra Junipers*
1936. Carbon pencil